Lewis Henry Steiner

The Genealogy of the Steiner Family

Lewis Henry Steiner

The Genealogy of the Steiner Family

ISBN/EAN: 9783741187629

Manufactured in Europe, USA, Canada, Australia, Japa

Cover: Foto ©ninafisch / pixelio.de

Manufactured and distributed by brebook publishing software (www.brebook.com)

Lewis Henry Steiner

The Genealogy of the Steiner Family

THE GENEALOGY OF THE STEINER FAMILY

ESPECIALLY OF THE DESCENDANTS OF

JACOB STEINER

BY

LEWIS H. STEINER, M. D.

AND

BERNARD C. STEINER, PH. D.

BALTIMORE
PRESS OF THE FRIEDENWALD CO.
1896

PREFACE.

Among the papers of my father, the late Lewis H. Steiner, were several pages of notes towards a genealogy of our family. These have been taken up and much amplified, and the work is now issued, as it is not likely that further delay would elicit many more facts of importance. It has been a pleasant task to me to search out the various branches of the family tree.

Almost all to whom application was made have been helpful; but especial thanks are due for time spent and interest shown in the work, to Miss Alice V. Derr, Mrs. Marcus A. Woodward, Miss Ola Michaels, Gen. John A. Steiner, Mr. Thomas C. Stoner, Mrs. Wm. H. Lewis, Miss Rachel L. Eader, Mr. Edward T. Schultz, Mr. John G. Wilson, Mr. Charles A. S. Steiner and Mr. Paul Wisenall. We have not been famous; but, to quote my father's words, we have been a " family whose members have lived and died as plain, honest, law-abiding, citizens."

BERNARD C. STEINER.

PART I.

SKETCHES FROM THE EARLY HISTORY OF THE STEINER FAMILY IN GERMANY.

(Translated by Lewis H. Steiner.)

The family arms of the family of Steiner von Steindorf consist of a silver shield, in the middle of which is displayed a red bear in an erect posture. A closed helmet covers the shield, having, as a crest, a red bear's head looking to the left. The ornaments of the arms consist of foliage, half red and half gold, the same being placed on a red stelle with small white pearls. Below the shield there sweeps a white band (Wappenband) with a red back, bearing the name Maxmylian Steiner in red ecclesiastical letters. The whole constitutes a true representation of the arms which Ludwig of Bavaria presented to the ancestor of the Steiner family at the tournament of Goslar.

The diploma of nobility, as well as the letters, which were confirmed by Emperor Sigismund in 1397 and announced at Erfurt, July 26, 1397, are to be found in the original in the Imperial Chamber at Wetzlar. A copy is in the archives of family arms (Familien-Wappen-Archiv) at Vienna.

The imperial archives of the nobility of the empire at Wetzlar, and registry office of family ancestry and arms at Vienna, contain, with reference to the origin of the noble family of *Steiner*, the following material, the correctness of which is made clear and evident by reference to the books of heraldry and tournaments at Speyer and Frankfort-on-the-Main.

These show that the family of Steiner appears for the first time as a noble house in one of the archives of the Reichskammer of the Elector of Saxony, which is dated " Regensburg, 22d of the month of August in the year of our Saviour 1340." As the cause of this record appear the decrees of the Criminal Court (Halsgerichtsordnung), from which it appears that Ludwig von Steindorf had been cited from his family seat at Steindorf in the Oberlausitz in consequence of a quarrel with Uffo von Bonkenburg, by the Superior Court at Regensburg, for a breach of the Landfriede, and that, through the management of Anselm, the Bishop of Würzburg, who was a brother of Uffo von Bonkenburg, he was placed under the imperial ban, and, in consequence of this, his family castle was confiscated and the possession of the same was adjudged to the complainant Uffo.

Ludwig von Steindorf went into a monastery at Goslar and died in the same, March 27, 1342, from grief and anguish at the rendition of so unjust a judgment. It appears that after some months, the Emperor, by a decree of December 31, 1341, three months *before the death* of the condemned, had annulled the imperial ban. But the edict was concealed and held back by the trickery of the revengeful Bishop of Würzburg, who bore the responsibility of the same readily on account of the great influence he possessed at court.

It appears from the records of this court that the father of Ludwig von Steindorf—the head of a family (Stammvater) so widely distributed—was named

I. MAXIMILIAN STEINER.[1]

He was made a knight (Ritter) on the 26th of November, 1311, by Ludwig of Bavaria. A singular occurrence was to be thanked for this good fortune. He was a squire (Knappe) of the Count of Mannsfeld, and saved the life of his royal highness, Ludwig of Bavaria, in a bear-hunt, having freed him from great peril of life by seizing a bear that rushed at him and strangling it with both hands. The king created him knight (Ritter) at Goslar, at the next tournament, and presented him with a silver armor (Rüstung) and a costly shield, the arms of which exhibited *a red bear* on a silver field. But as Maximilian was without property and possessed nothing besides his gigantic strength and bravery, his brave and fearless heart, his king and lord gave him a knight's castle which he had won from Günther, the Bishop of Würzburg, at (Brettspiele) draughts. This Maximilian made his family castle (Stammschloss), and changed its name from Günthersburg, which it had been called before, to Steindorf.

He married shortly afterwards Margaretha von Bassenheim, the daughter of his neighbor, Gottfried von Bassenheim. But in the midst of the happy days of his marriage, the duty of gratitude and the voice of his fatherland called him to the battle-field for his king. He collected from his neighborhood a small company (Fahnleinschaft) of 60 brave lancemen, and, as their captain (Feldhauptmann), fought under His Majesty Ludwig, and fell in the battle given against Frederick of Austria at Mühldorf at the head of his faithful followers. His widow renounced the pleasures of the world and entered the nunnery of Wunsiedl, known as Maria Schutz, where, in a short time, she gave birth to a son, to whom she gave, at baptism, the name of the king in whose cause her faithful spouse had fallen. Grief for her lost husband did not permit her to live to see the coming year, and she died, December 29, 1312.

Her only son,

II. LUDWIG,[2]

in accordance with the wish of his grandfather, was surrendered to the same, who managed also most faithfully his castle of Steindorf. But Ludwig had scarcely attained the age of youth when this grandfather, Gottfried von Bassenheim, died, and, as no other heirs had legal claims, the knight's estate of Bassenheim fell to him. Uffo von Bonkenburg set up unfounded and illegal claims to a part of the landed property belonging to Bassenheim, which Ludwig would not recognize. This state of affairs led to much quarrelling and contention. His antagonist at length knavishly played the part of peace-maker, and declared that all ill-will should be done away with and all claims be relinquished if Ludwig von Steindorf would marry Gertrude, the only daughter of Uffo. But Steindorf married a poor but virtuous maiden, the daughter of the sacristan (Küster) of the cathedral of Sancta Clara, and gave, as a bridal gift and as dower at the same time, the castle of Bassenheim with all its enclosures, grounds and cattle. From this time on the quarrel with his ancient and irreconcilable enemy broke out anew.

Ludwig's spouse, Adelgunde, bore him three sons—Ludwig, Bernhardt and Roland—and died at the birth of the last two, who were twins. As if anticipating her own death, she bequeathed to her children, two days before the day of their birth and her death, the castle of Bassenheim with all the grounds thereto belonging, by a will written by the abbess of the Sancta Clara Chapter. Her corpse was scarcely interred in the convent vault when Uffo von Bonkenburg once more broke his solemn oath with Ludwig von Steindorf, and he, the continual disturber of the Landfriede, relying on the power which, at that time, his brother Anselm, the Bishop of Würzburg, possessed with the court, stepped forth as complainant, knowing he could not affect his courageous opponent by force of arms. As was mentioned before, Ludwig lost, by the declaration of the imperial ban, his family possessions, and these fell, by the cunning influence of the Bishop of Würzburg, to his brother Uffo, whilst Ludwig died in the cloister. Before he had determined to carry out this so incomprehensible resolution—to terminate his life within the walls of a monastery—he committed the care of his children to the abbess of the neighboring convent of Sancta Clara, and the superintendence of their education to his tried friend Oscar Bentivoglio, whom he constituted guardian of the same, and who, for some years, had been castellan of the castle at Steindorf. He faithfully performed his duty as friend, and died at an advanced age, after he had experienced the pleasure of having the twins that had been entrusted to his care educated and accomplished in tournaments and the use of arms.

III. LUDWIG,'

the eldest of the sons, on the day of his wedding with Agnes von Hohenberg-Kolbina, gave his lawful name of Steindorf to the castle heretofore called Bassenheim. He had with his consort two daughters and one male heir,

VI. WILHELM,[1]

who studied jurisprudence in Worms, sold the castle of Steindorf and died unmarried.

The castle of Steindorf was afterwards owned by the Lord von Kitzbüchel, and was later, in the religious wars, entirely destroyed.

The name of the family Steiner was only perpetuated by Roland, as IV. Bernhardt[2] died without leaving male offspring by his spouse Octavia Fehland.

V. ROLAND STEINER[3]

filled the office, for some years in Speyer, of Stadthauptmann, a very respectable position sought after by many of the most patrician citizens. He was sent as deputy to the imperial election at Ghent, when Carl IV. was elected. The coronation took place in Aachen, and Roland was presented by the emperor with a gold chain of honor, to which his portrait was attached. He was immediately married to Conradine Schauenstein, to whom he had already been affianced. The burghers of the city gave him a banquet of honor, which was celebrated with princely splendor and lasted for three days. His offspring consisted of two sons and three daughters. He died in the year 1374, and his wife followed him in the same year.

VII. ALOYSIUS,[4]

the eldest son, withdrew from the world and took the place of monastery steward (Klostervogt) in Speyer. He married Gertrude von der Mühlen, the daughter of a Holland merchant, and met his death in 1403 in the waters of the Rhine, his boat, during a night passage, having been dashed on a concealed rock and sunk. He left two sons; a third, X. Johann or Hans by name, was abducted from the paternal mansion when a child without any one afterwards being able to secure information as to his enigmatical disappearance or his further fate.

IX. ANDREAS GOTTFRIED[5]

was the younger son, and died as Dean of the Cathedral in Mayence. He stood in high estimation on account of his learning, and was for a long time the right hand of the Archbishop.

VIII. THEODOR,[5]

the eldest son of Aloysius Steiner, married Antonia Splinter, and as even in his early years he showed a taste for military life, entered in the imperial service; fought later in the Hussitenkriege, and died in the year 1449, in a fall from his horse. He left behind three sons, who, on account of their numerous offspring, deserve to be called the proper (Stammhalter) heads of the Steiner family afterward so numerous.

XI. FRIEDERICH THEODOR,[6]

the eldest son, studied law in Vienna, entered into the Austrian imperial service, and was afterwards made Imperial Councillor (Kaisersrath). He married Maria Schweppe, daughter of the burgomaster at Vienna, and had four sons. After she died, in 1460, Friederich married the young widow Amalie, Baroness von Einsiedel, who bore him five other sons, named XIII. Ernst,[7] XIV. Julius,[7] XV. Ludwig,[7] XVI. Winfried[7] and XVII. Christian;[7] Ernst and Julius entered the army, the others and XVIII. Friederich,[7] XIX. Johann[7] and XX. Leopold,[7] of the first marriage, dispersed to Bavaria, Suabia, and on the Rhine, so that we are unable to find any further connected information about them.

XII. GEORG[6]

was the younger brother of Friederich Theodor, and the second son of Theodor; he entered the service as page (Leibpage) at the court of "Charles the Bold"—Duke of Burgundy, and as the latter made him a knight, he remained in his train. He married Elisabeth Durand, the daughter of a rich merchant of Ghent, and perished at the battle of Nancy, 1477. He left three small sons, XXII. Georg,[7] XXIII. Ludwig[7] and XXIV. Herrmann,[7] who moved with their mother to Ghent.

XXIX. WILHELM,[6]

the youngest son of Theodor, remained in Speyer; owned a very extensive commercial business, and was the president (Vorstand) of the Merchants' Guild. His wife, Isabella Horst, lamented for years the loss of her husband, who died, in consequence of a cold, on his return from a business excursion to the Netherlands, at Aachen, in 1480, leaving two sons,

XXX. ADOLF[1] AND XXXI. MARTIN.[1]

The former died some weeks after his marriage. Martin, having learned the business of goldsmith, went to Coblentz and settled there as a jeweller. On a journey to Suabia, Leopold Bernauer released him from the hands of highway robbers, who attacked him with the view of plunder. He formed the most intimate friendship with his deliverer, purchased a small estate for him, and married his sister Amalie, to whose family the celebrated Agnes Bernauer, who met an unfortunate death in the Donau, belonged. Martin ofterwards went to Brazil and enriched himself in the then newly-discovered diamond diggings. Shortly after his return he died in 1498, and left his large family considerable possessions. (This story is, of course, incorrect, but I know not how to correct it.—B. C. S.) He had five sons— Martin,[5] Albert,[6] Friedrich,[7] Moritz[8] and Adalbert.[9]

XXXII. MARTIN[5]

was established as a goldsmith in Nürnberg, where he died, 1509, a mysterious death, and when his corpse was examined it appeared that he had been poisoned. Very weighty and unequivocal grounds of suspicion rested on his wife, who had had secret intercourse with a Doctor Bonefacius, who was universally feared in Nürnberg. Public opinion designated him as a magician, and every one shunned his neighborhood. But satisfactory evidence could not be produced; even the application of torture wrung no confession from her. She was banished by public opinion from the country; all the costly stones and ingots of gold secretly put away by her at the death of her husband were taken from her and she was driven over the borders. The people attacked the house of the doctor, tore it down, burnt the great books out of which he, as they asserted, invoked the evil spirits, and hunted him with dogs from the precincts of the imperial city. Martin left a son —XXXVII. Gotthardt[9]—who, however, died before he had attained his majority. The very considerable property left behind melted away under the fearful law costs, which were only terminated after 60 years, during which more than 30 Steiners von Steindorf, male and female bearers of the name, were claimants for the treasures of the inheritance.

XXXIII. ALBERT[8]

lived first in Frankfort-on-the-Main, and came to Cologne-on-the-Rhine, where he died, 1516. He left seven sons and five daughters, of whom the former, after the death of their father, mostly left Cologne without our being able to give an account of them. XXXVIII. Markus[9] Edler was one of them.

XXXIV. FRIEDRICH[8]

had early studied theology at Meissen and distinguished himself by his spirited defense of the principles of the Lutheran faith at the Diet called by the Elector John of Saxony at Schmalkalden. He died in Meissen, having only one son, Oswald,[9] who dedicated himself likewise to the theological profession, and, while pastor in Lützen, was killed in a revolt of the peasants.

XXXV. MORITZ[8]

entered into military service after he had squandered his estate in Italy. He stood in great favor with the Princess of Anhalt, and very different accounts were given in those days of the nature of the connection in which he stood to her. He had many love intrigues, through which he was involved almost weekly in duels, but always came off victor. In the battle of Pavia, 1525, he very particularly distinguished himself, and it was attributed principally to him that the king, Francis I., was taken in the same. He married Bianca Graselli of Brescia, celebrated for her beauty, and from that time forward changed his dissolute mode of life. He lived several years in Lothringen and died, 1555, at Colmar, where he had been a widower for four years before his death. He left four sons, concerning whose career no records are left.

XXXVI. ADALBERT[8]

was the youngest brother, and Consistorialrath in Augsburg. From the deepest and most sincere conviction of evangelical truth, went to Wittenberg; was a friend of Luther's, and was in correspondence with him long afterwards, when he returned to Augsburg. He contributed very much towards the religious peace determined at Nürnberg, 1552, and was, until his death, the court theologian (Hoftheologe) of Moritz of Saxony. He fell in the last capacity in the battle of Seivorshausen, in 1554, leaving five sons, Adalbert,[9] Johann,[9] Carl,[9] Leopold[9] and Adolph.[9] The first two settled at Tübingen; Carl died without male offspring in Würzburg, and the younger brothers died without our being able to find anything further about them, notwithstanding the zealous searches of their brothers. Nothing is extant also with reference to the families of the two eldest.

Hitherto we have only been able to give the succession of the heads of the Steiner family; the following notices are with reference to separate persons, but are based on personal searches.

XVIII. FRIEDRICH VON STEINER[7]

was professor of medicine in the university founded at Tübingen on October 9, 1477, by Count Eberhardt mit dem Bart. He was afterwards rector of this high school, and died in 1491. He left only two sons, but many daughters. From his family papers, which were in possession of his sons, it appeared that he was a son of Friederich Theodor Steiner von Steindorf. Both of his children, one of whom was named

XXVII. HUGO,[8]

lived for some years in Tübingen, which is all that is known of them. His name does not appear on the baptismal register, whence it is to be supposed that they were not born in Tübingen. Their mother died some years before their father.

There lived in Fulda, quite retired from the world, an old man, concerning whose family no one had any knowledge. He died in 1479 and left a considerable estate. He was in possession of a small house, never suffering himself to be seen, and holding no communication with his fellow-men, appearing to live as though he had an aversion to the living. He gave no alms to the poor, and was only known by the name of "der alte Steinmarder." It was discovered after his death that his name was

X. HANS VON STEINER,[5]

and that he had been enticed away from his parents' house by a woman when a boy five years old and taken to Poland. Here he was educated and travelled to Palestine, Jerusalem, Egypt, from whence, thirty years before his death, he came to Fulda and lived secluded from the world. Who removed him from his father's house, if he ever had a wife, whence came his wealth, why he shunned mankind with so much enmity, and why he never returned to his home,—a veil enshrouded these questions and no one ever learned the answer to them. He owned many Eastern manuscripts which no one could understand. It is an undeniable fact that he was the son of Aloysius Steiner—the Klostervogt who died in 1403—who, when a child at Speyer, had disappeared in so mysterious a manner. As Hans von Steiner died without a will, considerable property fell to the exchequer, since no heirs appeared.

In 1520, forty years after this, there arrived at Fulda a (Rittersmann) young knight,

XLI. LUDWIG VON STEINER,[*]

and proved from his baptismal certificate (Taufschein) and other documents that he was a relative of the deceased Hans von Steiner, and then instituted a process for the inheritance so long unclaimed. Some of the most distinguished jurists appeared on his side, but that which the exchequer ever seizes is not given up for slight reasons. Ludwig carried his case to the Emperor, Charles V., at the Imperial Diet of Worms. We learn that Ludwig himself was afterwards murdered, and the suit thus naturally came to an end. With reference to the mode of his death, the following appears in an old chronicle of Worms. At Worms, at the Imperial Diet, which was opened April 18, 1521, a Ludwig Steiner von Steindorf was present, who was so transported by the defense of Luther that he embraced Luther, and, in the fullness of his conviction, cried out: "Man of God! from now on shall my heart and my sword hearken unto thy doctrines, and may I be condemned (verflucht soll Ich sein) if I do otherwise than I say and feel!" Two days later Ludwig was found with five stabs in his body, murdered on his bed at the inn, and his corpse was denied a lodgment in consecrated ground. From various letters and other papers it appeared that his grandfather was XI. Friedrich Theodor[6] von Steiner—the Rathsherr who died at Vienna, May 3, 1468—and that his father lived in Torgau. He had six brothers and four sisters; of the former nothing definite is known, excepting of one, a true adherent of Sickingen,

XLII. BERNHART VON STEINER.[5]

It is known that this one was a brother of the murdered Ludwig, and that Bernhart fell—1523—by the side of Sickingen, who was shot in his castle of Landstuhl when beleaguered by the Elector of Treves.

XXII. GEORG TRAUGOTT STEINER.[7]

A cathedral scholastic, was for many years in the Chapter at Regensburg and died there, 1522. It was ascertained from his papers that he was the eldest son of XII. Georg von Steindorf,[6] who fell in the fight at Nancy, and that his two brothers, XXIII. Ludwig[7] and XXIV. Herrmann,[7] lived in Aschaffenburg. Ludwig was City Syndic (Stadtsyndicus) at that place and afterwards Burgomaster of Aschaffenburg. Herrmann was the head manager (Oberverwalter) of the possessions of Thurn and Taxis. From the church records it is seen that Ludwig had no male heirs; Herrmann, however, had two sons, of whom Carl,[8] the elder, died when a boy, and the younger, whose name was

XXVI. HEINRICH,[8]

moved to Nürnburg and there became a merchant. In the church books of that place is found the record of his wedding day, when he married Kunigunda Gebhardt of Anspach; he permitted his spouse, however, in a few weeks to separate from him, because he went over to the Evangelical confession of faith. He had no children, and, moreover, did not marry again. He was forced to take refuge in flight—1582—with many others, in consequence of animosities. Nothing further was heard of him, and his very large property was confiscated.

The Margrave of Anspach had a physician-in-ordinary by the name of

XXXVIII. MARKUS[8] EDLER VON STEINER,

who often declared that his grandmother was the sister of the celebrated Agnes Bernauerin, but he was in possession of no particular account of his family, and only knew that his father had died at Cologne in 1516. When Markus von Steiner died, it was discovered from his papers that he had several brothers, of whom two lived in Regensburg; another, XXXIX. Thomas[9] in Zweibrücken and XL. Reinhardt[9] Steiner in Strasburg, the last one being likewise a doctor, and many letters were found from him. We conclude from these facts that Markus was one of the sons of XXXIII. Albert von Steiner[8] and a grandson of XXXI. Martin[7] Steiner, who died at Coblentz. During the religious wars, and particularly the Thirty Years War, many of the Steiner descendants were driven from their estates, and, in those times, most of the records and church registers were destroyed in the pillaging and conflagrations of the churches and town-houses, whence also many genealogical tables were destroyed or made defective.

At the siege of Magdeburg, under General Tilly, and the massacre connected with it, May 10, 1631,

XLIII. ERNST VON STEINER,[10]

a prominent burgher and Rathsassessor, came to his end in a terrible manner. He was suspected of being a Protestant, and the brutal Walloons literally quartered him, his head was stuck on a halberd, which was planted with a great many others before the town-house. The slaughter was so terrible that of 38,000 inhabitants scarcely 5000 were left alive. The wife of the murdered man saved nothing but her life, and fled, after an infant had been torn from her breast and stabbed before her eyes, with the four remaining children. Nothing further is known of the unhappy family. Some of the old burghers said that the grandfather of Ernst von Steiner had lost his life in a horrible way in Worms, so that it is to be presumed that this Ernst was a descendant of one of the six sons of XLI. Ludwig[*] von Steiner, who, during the Imperial Diet at Worms, in 1521, was assassinated.

From some Swedish sources, as well as from extracts of chronicles, which different students of history had collected, there are old manuscripts in the archives of Vienna which date 1640, 1642, 1645, wherein several Steiners von Steindorf are mentioned, who fought in the Swedish army under Gustavus Adolphus against Germany, being driven by a detestable persecution to this course. Indeed, it is founded on history that the so-called "Blauen Dragoner"—an universally feared regiment of horse—was commanded and led by a German named

WINFRIED[12] VON STEINER.

When Wallenstein, in 1628, made a fruitless attack on Stralsund, the same Winfried, whom the Swedes, from this time on, called the "Deutschen Eisenfresser," fell in such a manner upon the flank of Wallenstein's army, that the soldiery, otherwise so victorious, were obliged to enter upon a swift retreat, and in a renewed attack were completely put to flight with great loss. The same regiment, under the command of Winfried, who bore the title of a Field-Colonel (Feldobersten), in an invasion of Upper Silesia, took a large number of prisoners. A foolhardy leader of a small but courageous band rushed upon Winfried, and, notwithstanding the smallness of his squad, the former was cut to pieces in a moment, and its leader, accompanied by a few, was forced, with desperate opposition, even to the outside of the camp of the enemy. When he had succeeded in getting within sword's reach, the leader threw the murderous weapon that he had drawn on the chief away from him and threw himself in the arms of his parent with the exclamation: "Great God! my father!" It was

FRIEDRICH VON STEINER,[13]

the son of Winfried. There live at present, both in Stockholm and Nykiöbing, in Sweden, several families which have descended from this period. Winfried died in 1650 at Stockholm in very prosperous circumstances, and left only one son—Friedrich. Notwithstanding his zealous investigations as to the fate of his other two sons—Johann and Heinrich—who had been left in Germany, nothing could be learned. Winfried at the close of this mischievous war took a journey to Hahnheim at Amberg in Luzern, where he owned large estates, but the whole Steiner family, which had existed there, was deceased, and the mournful mounds which he met there were the only sad testimonies of their former happy past. An only daughter, who was married to a butcher (Metzger) named Huber, who had perished likewise in the desolations of the war, he found at Baireuth, and she asserted that both her brothers, Johann and Heinrich, were killed in the Saxon battles. Winfried returned to Sweden without being able to bring along with him satisfactory information as to his relatives. So much is only known of his own descent, that he was descended from XXXIII. Albert von Steiner,[5] who was his great-great-grandfather. Winfried's father was Johann,[14] and was established in Tübingen, where he died in 1604, and Winfried acted as merchant in Amberg after his father's death.

Friedrich, his son, married a Swede and had several children, whose descendants still live in Sweden. A Steiner possesses at present important iron-works in that country, and has considerable commercial transactions with Russia and England.

At the end of the Thirty Years' War, whose bloody effects left traces for more than half a century afterwards, a general census was taken in Germany, and it appears from various summaries and registers that there then lived, 1652, in the German States, 94 male and 109 female owners of the name of Steiner von Steindorf.

The desolation produced by the French towards the end of the

THE GENEALOGY OF THE STEINER FAMILY. 19

17th century, and especially the invasions into the Rhinelands in 1686, called forth such horrors as all wars are accompanied with. Among the unfortunate who lost their property and estates and were obliged to seek their safety in flight were to be found many descendants of the Steiner family; many of these fled to Switzerland, and at the present time some of this family still live there.

Furthermore, these are to be met with very numerously in Bavaria, Würtemburg, Saxony, Rhine-Prussia and in the Austrian monarchy; but the numerous researches which have been conducted by separate members of the Steiner family can detect no connected line of descent, as most of these had lost their records in the war periods since 1625. It appears from old documents that many of the Steiner family living in the Rhine Palatinate, as well as in Austria and Steiermark, at the end of the last century or the beginning of this, emigrated to America.

The separate notices which have been collected together in this narrative are partly the result of labor and investigations into extracts from old documents and family papers, into verbal copies of chronicles where descendants of the Steiner family are named. They relate to persons who have been prominent, although it is further known that many unfortunate members of the Steiner family, in consequence of misfortune, have been forced to occupy themselves with agriculture and have lived in the darkness of obscurity.[1]

Between the years 1680 and 1685 there lived a large number of the Steiner family scattered about in the Rhine Palatinate, at Worms, in the country along the Neckar and in Hesse. But when the horrible devastations of the French threw the firebrand of bloody war among the peaceful provinces, when the castle of Heidelberg was blown into the air, Worms and Speyer burnt, and murder, robbery and pillage drove thousands of families away, then the Steiner family also was so scattered that any further connected account of it cannot be given.

Many Germans from the different crown-lands of the monarchy wandered into Austria under the Empress Maria Theresa,

---

[1] These facts were prepared from the records in Germany for Mr. Jacob Steiner of Philadelphia about 1855.

as well as under the government of Joseph II., and also from Würtemburg to Hungary, where several families yet live having the name of Steiner. From partial notices which have been handed down from children to children, as well as from genealogical tables found in a Bible which had been owned for over 200 years by a Steiner family, it is to be concluded that most of the owners of this name were descendants of Rathsherr Friedrich Theodor von Steiner, who died in Vienna, 1468. But the most of these had emigrated from necessity and during the war periods, and under no prosperous circumstances, partly country people or mechanics, who were securing for themselves a new asylum by their activity and diligence.

PART II.

EARLY STEINER SETTLERS IN AMERICA WHO MAY HAVE BEEN RELATED TO JACOB STEINER.

Christian Steiner[1] was naturalized October 14, 1729. He bought land in Strasburg Township, Lancaster County, Pennsylvania, and built a mill there, which, in 1730, was one of three in the county. He also kept a house of entertainment and sold rum "by the small." He came to this country[2] as early as 1720.

In his will[3] he is described as of Lampeter Township, yeoman. He gave his son Christian his mills and divided his land at "Conawagga," York County, equally among all his children. Either the father or son of the name Christian[4] sold land in 1750 and 1763. He mentions sons Jacob, John and Christian in his will, dated September 30, 1758.

Abraham Steiner[5] settled in Lancaster County and had land granted him on October 7, 1735, and in Lebanon Township received a grant of other land[6] on December 12, 1739. His wife was Mary ———. She gave bond as administratrix[7] of his estate in 1741, and put in a final account on June 10, 1743. He was never naturalized.[8] His wife could not write. His son Abraham married Salome ——— and removed to Bethlehem, Northampton County.[9] He sold land in Lancaster County in 1762. Both he

[1] Rupp, Lancaster Co., pp. 77, 126, 254.
[2] Rupp's Collection of 30,000 Names, p. 353.
[3] Lancaster County Will Book B, Vol. 1, p. 271.
[4] Recorder's Office, 1750, and Vol. H, p. 136.
[5] Patent Book A, Vol. 7, p. 95. Recorded in Harrisburg.
[6] Patent Book A, Vol. 10, p. 23.
[7] Register's Office, Lancaster.
[8] Recorder's Office. Book H, p. 43.
[9] Patent Book AA, Vol. 3, p. 197 (in Harrisburg); Recorder's Office, Vol. M, pp. 252, 391. Three deeds, one recorded in 1767 and one in 1768.

and his wife wrote in German script. By trade he was a blacksmith.

In 1755, John Stoner, miller, sells land in Lancaster County to John Newcomer.

In 1756, John Stoner, of "Connestogoe," having died, his children execute a deed of partition of the father's land. Their names were Abram (described as yeoman), Christian, Catharine and John.

Abraham Steiner[1] bought 63 acres of land on Conestoga Manor, Lancaster County, on May 3, 1740, and 200 acres in 1762. In the same place Christian Steiner bought 244 acres in 1761.

Christian[2] or Christopher Steiner, a blacksmith, had house in Fredericktown in 1768.

John, David, and Abraham Steiner,[3] described as farmers, and as of Antrim Township, Cumberland County, Penn., owned land in Frederick County. Their wives were respectively Catharine ———, Margaret ——— and Mary ———. John had a son of the same name, who was described as his heir in 1771, and was then unmarried.[4] David and Abraham, with their wives, were alive[5] in 1772. John Sr. sold land called Egypt on the north side of Antietam Creek near Steiner's Mills as early as March 18, 1750.[6]

Jacob Steiner,[7] of Anne Arundel County, bought Spring Garden, in Frederick County, in 1765, and had some connection with a John Steiner[8] in 1773.

Christian Steiner, yeoman of Hellam Township, York County, Penn., probably son of Christian, of Lancaster County, sold land

---

[1] Rupp's Lancaster Co., pp. 131, 132.

[2] L 322, M 45, Frederick Co. Records. Where the place of records is not given hereafter, Frederick County is to be understood.

[3] F 22, L 537, Frederick Co. Records.

[4] O 290, Frederick Co. Records.

[5] P 22, Frederick Co. Records.

[6] B 352, Frederick Co. Records.

[7] J 1053, Frederick Co. Records.

[8] P 624, Frederick Co. Records.

there on February 2, 1765,[1] and December 7, 1768, and bought land, August 1, 1763. His wife was Anna Maria ———. His will is dated June 17, 1786;[2] refers to slave Henry, whom he directs to be freed at the age of 25. Wife survived him. He is also referred to as Christopher.

Isaac Stoner lived in Manchester Township, York County, about the same time and had a wife, Anna ———. He sold land on April 5, 1764.[3]

[1] Record Book, Lancaster. Deeds, D 381, 383, C 260.
[2] Lancaster Will Book G, 115.
[3] York Record Book, B 340.

PART III.

JACOB STEINER, OF FREDERICK COUNTY, MARYLAND, AND HIS DESCENDANTS.

1. Jacob Stoner, or Steiner, was born ———, 1713, and died 1748, according to the dates on a tombstone in the old German Reformed graveyard in Frederick, which stone is probably that of our ancestor. It is quite probable that he was the Jacob Steiner who arrived at Philadelphia in the vessel Pennsylvania, Merchant, from Rotterdam on Sept. 11, 1731 (Rupp's List, p. 20). He had settled in Frederick County before 1736. On June 11 of that year Benjamin Tasker covenanted to convey a tract of land known as Tasker's Chance, lying on the Monocacy, to Abraham Miller, Daniel France, John George Lay, Joseph Smith, Peter Laney and Jacob Stoner for the sum of two thousand pounds. They were unable to raise the money and the sale fell through. In 1744 Daniel Dulany bought Tasker's Chance, probably as agent and attorney for the actual settlers. On July 28, 1746, Dulany transferred to the settlers most of the tract, on which he had laid out the town of Frederick. Jacob Stoner received the following tracts: "The Barrens," 103 acres for 25 pounds, beginning 160 perches from the Monocacy; "Indian Field," 202 acres for 15 pounds; "Mill Pond," 292 acres, on the Tuscarora Creek where it empties into the Monocacy, where Jacob Stoner's house and mill were; and "Bear's Den," or "Durburg," on the Tuscarora below "Mill Pond," 172½ acres, 25 pounds. The last two tracts adjoined the lands of Stephen Ramsburg and Abraham Miller. In 1742 he signed a petition to have Prince George parish divided and a new one established. He was evidently a man of some means and prominence in the community. He left no will and his estate was never administered upon (Land Records J, 1193, W. R. 17, 234, L. 1). He married ——— on ———. Jacob Steiner's land was divided in 1767. If we assume this was done at the attaining majority of his youngest son, Benedict, which is quite probable, we shall have Benedict as born in 1746.

Children of Jacob Steiner[1] and ——— ———:

2. John Steiner,[2] b. ———, 17— (5). d. Sept., 1798.
3. Henry Steiner,[2] b. ———, 17— (16). d. Sept., 1780.
4. Benedict Steiner,[2] b. ———, 17— (18). d. Sept., 1796.

THE GENEALOGY OF THE STEINER FAMILY. 25

2. Captain John Stoner,[2] or Steiner, married Catharine Elizabeth Ramsburg ———, 175—. She was born June 29, 1739, and died Jan. 29, 1792.

He inherited from his father the Mill Pond estate and carried on the business of a miller, while conducting farming operations at the same time. He was very successful and possessed a large fortune for those days.

Family tradition has reported that he was a soldier in the French and Indian war. Col. F. B. Steiner states that in 1838 he was told by an old Revolutionary soldier, then ninety-six years of age, that Capt. Stoner served in Braddock's campaign and that he was in the quartermaster's department of the Continental Army during the Revolution. He was a prominent citizen, being captain of militia in 1775. He served as a member of the Committee of Observation for the Middle District of Frederick County.

On November 2, 1779, he was one of the bondsmen of the sheriff of the county.

He probably was somewhat older than his brothers, and is said to have brought up them, as well as the only son of his brother Henry.

He first appears on the land records of Frederick County on August 19, 1767, when he divides his father's land, and is described as "miller, son and heir of Jacob Stoner" (L. 1). He also appears on the same day in connection with his brothers Benedict (K. 1435) and Henry (L. 2). His chief property, Mill Pond, was situated on Tuscarora Creek, and his mill was probably situated where Worman's Mill now stands, about ——— miles north of Fredericktown on the ——— road. Thence he rode into town, transacted business, and attended the German Reformed Church, of which the most of the family have been members.

On October 13, 1770, he bought Knave's Disappointment, situated in Georgetown, now in the District of Columbia (N. 401). Three years later, he and his neighbor and father-in-law, Stephen Ramsburg, agreed that over Ramsburg's land, known as Mortality, John Stoner might continue to carry his mill-race and water-course, carrying water from the Tuscarora Creek to his mill. He paid £10 currency for this privilege, and agreed to provide flood-gates and to keep the race in repair to prevent any injury to Ramsburg's land. Both parties bind themselves to keep the contract under penalty of £100. The whole proceeding is evidently a friendly one to prevent possible future "controversies and disputes" (V. 2). With Ramsburg and others, he joins in a petition on November 22, 1781, to have their bounds perpetuated (W. R. 2, 1083), and again five years later he petitions for the same thing (W. R. 6, 407).

In 1787, Capt. Stoner considerably enlarged his estate by buying portions of the confiscated property of Dulany (W. R. 7; 551, 650). He owned now land down to the Monocacy, and indeed on both sides of the stream. Between the banks of the Monocacy he conducted a ferry, adding this to his other occupations. Three years later he bought still more of the Dulany estate (W. R. 9, 258). He was now a large landowner; but he was getting old, and, in 1792, the loneliness of his advancing years was increased by his wife's death.

On Dec. 3, 1792, nearly a year after his wife's death, he began to dispose of his lands (W. R. 11, 232), and on May 4, 1795, he bought a lot on Second Street in Fredericktown (W. R. 13, 239), possibly moving there for his last years. A month later he made his last purchase of land (W. R. 13, 384), buying "Caspar's Inheritance." He sold land near the Mill Pond estate on June 16, 1796 (W. R. 14, 304). On Feb. 26, 1798, he sold at auction much of his farm equipment, disposing of two good mares, a number of sheep, steers and hogs, a negro boy, a good wagon and gears, an excellent house clock, and a variety of farming utensils (Bartgis's Federal Gazette). During the summer of 1798 his strength was gradually failing. On Aug. 23 he made his will. It is a rather long one, and disposes of personal property found by the executors to amount to £6999 17s 9d, a sum, roughly speaking, equal to $20,000, a very large estate for that time and place. The will is one that exhibits its maker in a favorable light. While stating he is of sound and disposing mind, he interjects, "Praised be God for it." He was a slaveholder, as most men of means then were; but was evidently a merciful master, for he directs all his "children to contribute equally towards maintaining and supporting my old negro woman, named Fan, during her life, as she is old and infirm and, at present, incapable of supporting herself." His negro man, Frank, about twenty-five years old, he gives to his son Henry, who has already been using his services; but, when Frank arrives at the age of thirty-two, "he shall be free and emancipated from slavery." A negro girl, Sally, aged eleven, is given to his daughter, Catharine Derr, and a negro boy, Bill, aged five, to his son Stephen.

The personal estate is directed to be sold by the executors, who were his sons Henry and Stephen. They were also to sell part of the land bought from the Dulany estate, to pay any debts he might have. The property was to be divided equally among his seven surviving children. The five children of his eldest son John, who had recently died, were to receive the share of their father, less £618, which had been advanced their father during his life. Their property was to be turned over to them as they reached the age of twenty-one. In the distribution of the estate it was found that each of the surviving children received £833 5s 7d, and each of the five children of John £43 1s 1½d currency.

A few days before making the will, he transferred his town house to his son Stephen (W. R. 17, 201), and a week after it, on Aug. 29, 1798, he sold for £5247, to William Potts, the Mill Pond estate, the rights over Ramsburg's land, the ferry, with an acre of ground across the Monocacy, where it landed, and a portion of the land confiscated by the State from Dulany. It will be thus seen that John Stoner had turned most of his

THE GENEALOGY OF THE STEINER FAMILY.   27

property into personalty. He lived only a few days after this last sale, and was dead before September 10, when his executors brought the will into the Orphans' Court.

The estate was not settled until June 10, 1802. We find the personal property had been sold at auction for £500 4s 1d. John Buckias received £2 12s 6d for "crying the sale," and Philip Rohr £1 17s 6d for acting as clerk at the sale. Dr. John Tyler had been paid £5 for attendance on Capt. Stoner, and Dr. Lewis Weltzheimer 6s 8d for drugs and medicines. Conrad Doll made the coffin for the burial for £4 10s (high price as compared with others), George Littlejohn received £1 for shaving Capt. Stoner after death, and Adam Strickstuck dug his grave for 15s. Capt. John Stoner was an ancestor of whom we may well be proud; a faithful, conscientious, honored, Christian citizen.

Captain Stephen Ramsburg, the father-in-law of John Stoner, on July 28, 1746, bought "Mortality," 473 acres, part of Tasker's Chance, from Daniel Dulany, for 15 pounds. He bought on Oct. 1, 1753, from Daniel Dulany the estate of Dearbought, containing 307¼ acres. He paid £100 for it (Frederick Co. Land Records, E. 278). On July 3, 1755, he sold the property to Sebastian Derr, whose son John married a daughter of Capt. John Stoner (E. 764). On Aug. 25, 1758, he bought a tract of 100 acres, being part of Dulany's Lott (F. 566), and on Nov. 29, 1758, he bought 50 acres more of Dulany's Lott (F. 608). On May 11, 1761, he sold to Jacob Crist 190 acres of land on Ruess's (Reese's) Branch, which runs into the Monocacy (G. 6). He sold lots 28 and 29 in Fredericktown on July 14, 1761 (G. 106). These lots he bought from Daniel Dulany, and had his title confirmed to them by Dulany's executor on May 14 and June 23, 1762 (H. 51, 52, 82; G. 502).

He was a farmer and miller, and on Oct. 1, 1762, made an agreement with his neighbor William Durm with regard to a proposed mill-dam, which would cause the overflow of some of Durm's land. In return for the damage he agreed to pay £45 (H. 135). Shortly afterwards he served as executor for his friend Jacob Storm (J. 1184) and bought 114 acres of land, being the Resurvey on Nutt Spring (J. 1245). On Aug. 16, 1768, he sold the Resurvey on Stoney Hill and Shoemaker's Choice, comprising 111 acres (L. 398). On April 6, 1770, he sold his eldest son, John Ramsburg, for £250, the part of Dulany's Lott which he owned (L. 628). The second son, Jacob, received the remainder of his father's property in the Resurvey on Stoney Hill and Shoemaker's Choice on July 4, 1770 (N. 231). Fourteen years later, on Dec. 30, 1784 (W. R. 5, 271), he transferred part of Tasker's Chance, known as Mortality, comprising 62½ acres, to his third son, Elias Ramsburg.

His wife was Catharine Brunner, whom he must have married soon after 1730, who was alive in 1770, but dead before 1784. Their children were: John; Catharine Elizabeth, who married Captain John Stoner; Jacob; Elias; Anna Margaret, who married Christopher Myers, and was great-grandmother of Lewis H. Steiner; Henry; and Christian. He was for many years an elder of the Evangelical Reformed Church of Frederick, and as such bought land for the church (G. 368, J. 362, M. 43). In 1768, with the other elders, he made an agreement with Rev. Bennet Allen, Rector of All Saints parish, "for the more general comfort and edification of that part of the parishioners who are Germans." For this and other good causes and considerations and the sum of two shillings, Allen grants to the elders, while he shall be incumbent of All Saints, £25 current money, yearly, provided they apply it to the payment of a "minister that is received of and approved" by the Reformed Calvinists.

On Jan. 25, 1785, he manumitted (W. R. 5, 290) his negro slave Nan, aged about 40; John Stoner was witness to the deed. To the same woman, who took care of him during the last years of his life, he willed "the bed and bedding that she now uses at my house," and for "her past services and attention" he bequeathed her an annuity of £6 current money. Out of his personal estate £100 were to be reserved during her life for the payment of this annuity. His will was dated April 19, 1788, and describes him as "far advanced in years." He died on March 7, 1789, and on March 21 the will was presented for probate. He signed his name to it in German script. He left his son John, whom he made executor, a tract of 27 acres in Washington County, known as Adventure, and a bond of £43 3s 1d due from Capt. John Stoner. He also gave him "my two negroe boys, named Jack and Bill, untill they arrive at the age of 26 years, at which ages respectively, I have by deed duly executed, acknowledged, and to be recorded, manumitted and set them free, the said devise and bequest of the negroes to John to be on the express condition that he, his executors or administrators, do and shall, before their arrival at the ages at which they are manumitted by deed as aforesaid, instruct or cause the said negroe boys to be instructed and taught some good trade, whereby they may be at those ages the better enabled to support themselves."

Christian, the youngest son, received the family bible and two tracts of land in Frederick County: one, Chestnut Hill, of 50 acres; and the other, Mortality, of 200 acres. In return for these he is to pay £150 to Catharine Stoner. She also to have the "use and labour of a negroe woman named Sarah, now 18 years old, untill the said negro shall arrive at the age of 24 years, at which period her manumission, by deed bearing equal date herewith," is to take place. Stephen Ramsburg was born Oct. 11, 1711, and died March 7, 1789. The residue of the personal estate is to be divided equally among the children. The final account of the executor was rendered Aug. 10, 1792. He stated the personal estate amounted to £434 10s 8d. He charged the estate, among other items, with the following: Coffin and sundries for the funeral, £7 3d; Lawrence Brengle, clerk of the vendue, £1 10s; Jacob Miller, crier at vendue, 15s; nine gallons rum for vendue, £1 13s 9d.

THE GENEALOGY OF THE STEINER FAMILY.

Mrs. Ramsburg was a daughter of Joseph Brunner, who came from Schiefferstadt in Germany on the ——— in ———, 1729. With him came his son-in-law Christian Getzendanner, who married Anna Barbara Brunner (Rupp, 30,000 Names, p. 16). Joseph Brunner settled on a tract of land of about 1000 acres, immediately west of the present town of Frederick. This tract he divided into four farms: for his four sons, Jacob, John, Elias, and Henry, so that each farm should cross Carroll Creek and afford access to that stream for watering the cattle. On Jan. 17, 1753, he transferred to his third son Elias the homestead "Sheverstadt," which he had purchased from Dulany on July 28, 1746, and on which the present house was probably already built. He probably died soon thereafter (Frederick Co. Land Records E., p. 68, 104).

Children of Capt. John Steiner[2] and Catharine Elizabeth Ramsburg:

5. Jacob Steiner,[3] b. ———, 175—. Unmarried. d. ———, 17—.
6. John Steiner,[3] b. Sept. 17, 1757 (30). d. Summer of 1797.
7. Henry Steiner,[3] b. ———, 1764 (37). d. Apr. 24, 1831.
8. Mary Steiner,[3] b. ———, 1765 (46). d. June 10, 1830.
9. Stephen Steiner,[3] b. ———, 1767 (51). d. Sept. 8, 1829.
10. Christian Steiner,[3] b. Feb. 22, 1772, bap. May 10, 1772. d. young in 177—.
11. Catharine Margaret Steiner,[3] b. Feb. 4, 1774, bap. Apr. 1, 1774 (55). d. Nov. 25, 1812.
12. Christian Steiner,[3] b. March 28, 1776, bap. Sept., 1776 (60). d. June 25, 1842.
13. Frederick Steiner,[3] b. ——— (61). d. Aug. 3, 1836.
14. Elizabeth Steiner,[3] b. ———, 1780 (70). d. Sept. 3, 1866.
15. Maria Magdalena Steiner,[3] (?) b. Sept. 24, 1780. d. young (if child of Capt. John and Catharine).

3. Henry Steiner[2] married Elizabeth Link on ———, 177—. He was brought up by his elder brother John, according to family tradition. On Aug. 19, 1767, John transferred to him Stoner's Chance, a tract of land on the Tuscarora (L. 2). A part, at least, of this land he sold to Balzer Getzendanner on Apr. 5, 1770, when he was still unmarried. He was a farmer. His brother John administered his estate, which amounted to £252 19s 3½d, of which personal property was worth £212 6s 5½d, and debts due the estate £40 12s 10d. From there being no distribution of the estate recorded, it is possible that his wife and daughter were already dead.

Children of Henry Steiner and Elizabeth Link:

16. Elizabeth Steiner,[3] b. July 16, 1772, bap. Aug. 10, 1772. d. young (?).

17. John Steiner,² b. Mch. 12, 1774 (80). d. Dec. 3, 1854.

4. Benedict Stoner,² or Steiner, married ¹Maria Sibilla Loy on ———, 177—, and ²Anna Barbara Thomas on ———, 1775. He was a farmer, and lived on an estate containing 250¼ acres on the Monocacy, about two miles from Fredericktown. Of his farm, about 90 acres were under cultivation, a good proportion was meadow land and the rest was heavily timbered. On the place was a large and never failing spring, and good apple and peach orchards. After his death the property was sold pursuant to a decree of court (Bartgis' Federal Gazette).
On Mch. 22, 1792, he bought a part of the tract known as Spring Garden (W. R. 10, 510).

The children of Benedict Steiner² and Maria S. Loy were:
18. ¹ Benedict Steiner,³ bap. May 10, 1772 (90). d. ———.
19. ² Mary Steiner,³ b. ———, 177— (91). d. ———.

The children of Benedict Steiner² and Anna B. Thomas were:
20. Elizabeth Steiner,³ b. May 7, 1776, bap. Oct. 1, 1776 (92). d. June 13, 1857.
21. Mary Magdalen Steiner,³ b. Feb. 22, 1778. d. Jan. 22, 1793.
22. Henry Steiner,³ b. Dec. 10, 1780, bap. Sept. 12, 1781 (94). d. ———.
23. Anna Barbara Steiner,³ b. Feb. 20, 1783 (95). d. Jan. 30, 1814.
24. Susanna Steiner,³ b. Nov. 25, 1785. Single. Lived with Jacob. d. Mch. 3, 1866.
25. Christian Steiner,³ b. ———. d. ———.
26. Jacob Steiner,³ b. Mch. 22, 1789 (98). d. Aug. 2, 1870.
27. David Eshebman Steiner,³ b. Oct. 23, 1790 (103). d. ———.
28. Christina Steiner,³ b. Oct. 23, 1790 (104). d. Feb. 19, 1866.
29. Charlotte Steiner,³ b. ———. d. ———, 1814.

6. John Steiner³ married Elizabeth Plank on June 27, 1785. She was born ———, 1755, and died Aug. 30, 1833. He studied medicine, and was known as "Doctor." He lived for a time in Virginia (father's will), and then in Creagerstown, where he probably died. His widow bought land in Creagerstown on May 15, 1798 (W. R. 16, 522). His brother Stephen was his administrator, and sold at auction, in Creagerstown, on Nov. 17, 1797, his household furniture, valuable mare, silver watch, joiner's and turner's tools, etc. His estate was not settled until May 17, 1802. He left a personal estate of £854 15s 1d. Of this the widow received £50 for education of the children after their father's death, and £260 as her portion, each child received £104.

Children of Dr. John Steiner³ and Elizabeth Plank:
30. Frederick Steiner,⁴ b. ———, 1786. Probably single. d. in Chambersburg, Pa.

THE GENEALOGY OF THE STEINER FAMILY.   31

31. David Steiner,⁴ b. Aug. 27, 1789 (107). d. May 21, 1868.
32. Infant daughter,⁴ b. ———, 179—. d. young.
33. Catharine Steiner,⁴ b. ———, 179—. d. infant.
34. Elizabeth Steiner,⁴ b. ———, 1792. Unmarried. d. ———, 1809.
35. Solomon Steiner,⁴ b. Mch. 15, 1796 (115). d. Nov. 26, 1856.
36. Hannah Steiner,⁴ b. Mch. 15, 1796 (121). d. Mch. 28, 1862.

7. Henry Steiner³ married Elizabeth Brengel Oct. 13, 1787. She was born Dec. 19, 1767, and baptized on May 29, 1768, and was the daughter of Jacob Brengel and Gertrude Bell. She died Apr. 17, 1833, leaving a personal estate of $190.52, which was swallowed up by debts. Henry Steiner by will left everything to his wife. He was a farmer, and lived on the Woodsborough road in Frederick County. He died in Frederick City (W. R. 9, 553). He was a dignified, quiet man.

Jacob Brengel probably married three times, the name of his first wife being unknown, and that of his third wife being Margaret. He married Gertrude Bell June 30, 1761. He was a farmer, and lived near Walkersville. He probably died in Jan., 1784, leaving a will and a personal estate of £495 17s 5d. Besides Mrs. Steiner, he had George and Christian, who settled in Kentucky; Lawrence, who became mayor of Frederick; and Catharine, wife of John Scholl. His third wife was probably a sister of the second, and both were probably children of John Bell, or Beall (Fred'k Land Records, Liber W. R. 2, 1073).

The children of Henry Steiner³ and Elizabeth Brengel were:
37. Ezra Steiner,⁴ b. June 22, 1788 (122). d. May 23, 1828.
38. Henry Steiner,⁴ b. Mch. 3, 1790 (127). d. Feb. 26, 1868.
39. Still-born son,⁴ b. Oct. 3, 1791. d. Oct. 3, 1791.
40. Elizabeth Steiner,⁴ b. Nov. 15, 1792. Single. Consumptive. d. May 11, 1830.
41. Jacob Steiner,⁴ b. Nov. 15, 1794 (137). Consumptive. d. Jan. 16, 1821.
42. Christian Steiner,⁴ b. Jan. 14, 1797 (138). d. Feb. 26, 1862.
43. John Steiner,⁴ b. Dec. 21, 1799. d. young.
44. Charity Steiner,⁴ b. Feb. 10, 1801. Single. Consumptive. d. Aug. 23, 1851.
45. Frederick Steiner,⁴ b. Mch. 13, 1803. A joiner. Lived in Washington, D. C. Single. A very handsome man. d. June 25, 1832.

8. Mary Steiner³ married Bernard Wiesenthal on Jan. 22, 1792. He was born ———, 1766, and died June 27, 1835. They lived at Shepherdstown, W. Va.

Their children were:
46. Henry Wiesenthal,⁴ b. ———, 179—. Single. Probably murdered on Ohio River near Guiandotte soon after 1834.

47. Elizabeth Wiesenthal,[4] b. Oct. 12, 1793 (142). d. Mch. 4, 1819.
48. Catharine Wiesenthal,[4] b. ———, 179— (142). d. ———, 1855.
49. Maria Wiesenthal,[4] b. Feb. 26, 1801. Unmarried. d. Jan. 8, 1820.
50. John Wiesenthal,[4] b. July 27, 1803 (142). d. Mch. 5, 1850.

9. Col. Stephen Stoner married [1] Barbara Ramsburg (born May 28, 1777, died March 7, 1820) on Oct. 11, 1795; [2] (widow) Elizabeth (Byerly) Bausman (born ———, 1788, died June, 1866) on ———, 1821. Col. Steiner was an architect, and built the steeple of the old German Reformed Church in Frederick in 1808 and the Stone Tavern in Bentztown (Frederick). His son, Mr. F. B. Steiner, states that he was told by Sergeant Lawrence Everhart that Col. Steiner, when 14 years of age, was of man's size and strength, and was enrolled as one of the guard over the Hessian prisoners, the most of the able-bodied men being absent from Frederick. In 1814 he raised the first company of volunteers in Western Maryland, and was attached with his company to the 16th militia regiment, Col. Ragan's. At the defeat of Bladensburg, Col. Ragan was wounded and taken prisoner. Col. Steiner then took command of the regiment. He was present with his troops at the battle of North Point, but was not brought into action.

Children of Col. Stephen Stoner[3] and Barbara Ramsburg:
51. George Stoner,[4] bap. Sept. 8, 1799. Single. d. in Frederick.
52. Charlotte Stoner,[4] b. Aug. 13, 1797 (145). d. Jan. 13, 1824.
53. Daniel Stoner,[4] b. Aug. 18, 1801 (145). d. ———, 1850, at Pittsburgh, Pa.

Child of Col. Stephen Stoner and Elizabeth Byerly:
54. Frederick Byerly Steiner,[4] b. May 28, 1822 (147).

11. Catharine Margaret Steiner[3] married John Derr on ———, 179—. He was a farmer and lived on the Monocacy, on the homestead he had inherited from his father. He was born ———, 1774, and died April 8, 1838.

Their children were:
55. Catharine Derr,[4] b. Apr. 28, 1797 (149). d. Nov. 9, 1884.
56. John Derr,[4] b. Nov. 28, 1798 (149). d. July 20, 1866.
57. Elizabeth Derr,[4] b. ——— (161). d. Aug. 3, 1883.
58. Mary Derr,[4] b. ——— (169). d. ———, 1860 (?).
59. Frederick Derr,[4] b. ———. Single. d. ———, 18—.

12. Christian Steiner[3] married, May 3, 1800, Susanna Ramsburgh (or Remsperger), daughter of George. She was born Mch. 8, 1782, and died

THE GENEALOGY OF THE STEINER FAMILY. 33

Aug. 8, 1857. They lived in Frederick City. Rev. Jno. Wm. Runkel married them.

Their child was:
60. William Christian Steiner,⁴ b. Jan. 2, 1812. d. Mch. 7, 1813.

13. Frederick Steiner³ was married to Margaret Sinn by Rev. Jno. Wm. Runkel on Feb. 15, 1800. She was born ———, 1782, confirmed in the Reformed Church in 1797, and died Jan. 19, 1857. He was confirmed in 1809 and was killed by a stroke of lightning in 1836.

Their children were:
61. Maria Steiner,⁴ b. Aug. 22, 1800 (180). d. ———, 18—.
62. John Frederick Steiner,⁴ b. Jan. 3, 1803. d. young.
63. Margaret Steiner,⁴ b. Nov. 1, 1803. d. young.
64. Frederick Steiner,⁴ b. Mch. 6, 1808 (joiner). Single. d. Aug. 24, 1836, in Frederick.
65. Jonathan Steiner,⁴ b. Oct. 20, 1810 (181). d. about 1884.
66. Jesse Steiner,⁴ b. Feb. 19, 1815 (182). d. Dec. 19, 1889.
67. Ann Elizabeth Steiner,⁴ b. July 24, 1816 (188). d. Oct. 29, 1878.
68. Joshua Steiner,⁴ b. Apr. 17, 1818 (189). d. Sept. 17, 1886.
69. Mary Margaret Steiner,⁴ b. Oct. 16, 1825. d. May 11, 1831.

14. Elizabeth Steiner³ married Sebastian Ramsburg on Nov. 16, 1800. He was born Aug. 18, 1779, and died Mch. 17, 1841.

Their children were:
71. Elias Ramsburg,⁴ b. Sept. 13, 1801. d. Aug. 17, 1802.
72. William Ramsburg,⁴ b. Aug. 24, 1803 (190). d. Jan. 7, 1869.
73. Mary Ramsburg,⁴ b. Oct. 21, 1805 (191). d. Sept. 26, 1826.
74. Catharine Ramsburg,⁴ b. Jan. 8, 1808 (192). d. July 5, 1831.
75. Sophia Ramsburg,⁴ b. Oct. 29, 1810 (192).
76. Elizabeth Ramsburg,⁴ b. Mch. 15, 1813. Single. Poolesville, Montgomery Co., Md.
77. Susanna Ramsburg,⁴ b. Mch. 2, 1816 (195).
78. Daniel T. Ramsburg,⁴ b. May 12, 1819 (198).
79. John H. Ramsburg,⁴ b. Nov. 19, 1821. Single. d. Sept. 16, 1842.

17. John Steiner³ married Susan Ramsburg Mch. 21, 1795. She died before reaching the age of forty. He lived as a farmer on the Monocacy until 1835, when he moved to Seneca County, Ohio, near Tiffin, where his farm was said to be a model one.

Their children were:
80. George W. Stoner,⁴ b. Dec. 12, 1795 (203). d. Oct. 2, 1884.

81. John Stoner,[4] b. May 27, 1798 (205). d. Jan. 28, 1827.
82. Ann Elizabeth Stoner,[4] b. Apr. 1, 1800. d. young.
83. Henry Stoner,[4] b. July 8, 1802. Killed by accident. Single. d. ———, 1820.
84. Christian C. Stoner,[4] b. Sept. 17, 1804 (207). d. Apr. 11, 1871.
85. Susanna Stoner,[4] b. Oct. 8, 1806 (211). d. Mch. 8, 1884.
86. Ann Rebecca Stoner,[4] b. June 12, 1808. Single. d. May 16, 1833.
87. Ann Elizabeth Stoner,[4] b. Aug. 20, 1812 (212). d. May 31, 1839.
88. Dennis Stoner,[4] b. ———, 181—. d. young.
89. Dennis Caspar Stoner,[4] b. Aug. 16, 1815 (213). d. Sept. 7, 1888.

18. Benedict Steiner[3] m. Kezia Morris, May 20, 1800.
90.

19. Mary Steiner[3] m. Abraham Faw on Mch. 16, 1788 [one account says Mch. 27, 1790].
91.

20. Elizabeth Steiner[3] m. David Eader of Frederick, Md., on Apr. 23, 1797 (b. Jan 30, 1774, d. Aug. 11, 1847).

Their children were:
92. Lewis Benedict Eader,[4] b. Apr. 23, 1798 (217). d. Jan. 2, 1873.
93. Eli Caspar Eader,[4] b. Dec. 4, 1808. d. Sept. 1, 1823.

21. Henry Steiner[3] m. Sarah Ragan, May 25, 1814.
94.

23. Anna Barbara[3] Steiner m. Thos. Derr, Apr. 10, 1803 (b. ———, 1779, d. Apr. 8, 1845). Lived in Frederick County until 1830, then in Tiffin, Seneca Co., Ohio.

Their children were:
95. Elizabeth Derr,[4] b. Jan. 1, 1804 (226). d. May 23, 1885.
96. Ezra Derr,[4] b. Jan. 1, 1807 (232). d. Jan. 30, 1890.
97. Margaret Derr,[4] b. Jan. 31, 1809 (239). d. Sept. 24, 1884.

26. Jacob Steiner[3] m. Mary Houck (b. Feb. 8, 1806, d. Sept. 25, 1888) on Oct. 25, 1829. He was a farmer, living near the Frederick City Reservoir.

Their children were:
98. Mary Ellen Steiner,[4] b. Aug. 26, 1830. d. Nov. 29, 1888.
99. Georgiana Steiner,[4] b. Feb. 23, 1833.

THE GENEALOGY OF THE STEINER FAMILY. 35

100. James Oliver Steiner,⁴ b. Feb. 23, 1835 (246). d. Oct. 16, 1894.
101. William Randolph Steiner,⁴ b. Nov. 8, 1839 (247).
102. Almedia Susan Steiner,⁴ b. Oct. 14, 1841.

27. David E. Steiner m. Catharine Bell on May 27, 1812.
103.

28. Christina Steiner³ m. Frederick Hauser, of Allegany Co., Md.

Their children were:
104. Anna Steiner Hauser,⁴ b. ———, 18—(248). d. ———.
105. Marion Hauser,⁴ b. ———, 18—. Unmarried. Lived in Garrett Co. d. ———, 18—.
106. Almedia Steiner Hauser,⁴ b. ———, 18— (252).

31. David Stoner⁴ married Ann Broadhead Stall on May 16, 1816. He was a farmer and lived at Toby Creek, Clarion Co., Pa. She was born Dec. 29, 1798, and died Dec. 29, 1880.

Their children were:
107. Margaret Elizabeth Stoner,⁵ b. May 11, 1818 (254).
108. Susannah Stoner,⁵ b. Mch. 21, 1821 (254).
109. John Wesley Stoner,⁵ b. Oct. 11, 1823 (258).
110. Caroline Stoner,⁵ b. Apr. 11, 1826 (263).
111. Hannah Maria Stoner,⁵ b. Aug. 19, 1829 (265).
112. Thomas Stall Stoner,⁵ b. June 12, 1832 (267).
113. Heiner Augustus Stoner,⁵ b. Dec. 5, 1834 (274). d. Dec. 2, 1889.
114. Flavius Josephus Stoner,⁵ b. Apr. 5, 1839. Unmarried. Lives at Arcota, Humboldt Co., Cal.

35. Solomon⁴ Stoner m. ¹Margaret Wolfe (b. Dec. 30, 1807, d. July 26, 1847) on July 21, 1829; ²Susan E. Garrard (b. July 27, 1814, ———) on Aug. 9, 1848. He resided at Pittsburgh, Penn., and was a prosperous merchant there.

Children of Solomon Stoner and Margaret Wolfe:
115. Elizabeth⁵ Stoner, b. Apr. 21, 1831 (278). d. June 5, 1883.
116. Catharine Wolfe⁵ Stoner, b. July 3, 1833 (280).
117. James Madison⁵ Stoner, b. Feb. 28, 1836 (289).
118. Victoria⁵ Stoner, b. Apr. 18, 1839 (297).
119. Alfred Montrose⁵ Stoner, b. Feb. 7, 1842 (297).
120. Anna Margaret⁵ Stoner, b. Oct. 10, 1845 (298).

36. Hannah Steiner⁴ m. Thomas Rowe on Apr. 24, 1828. He lived in Pittsburg, Pa., and died Oct. 15, 1837.

Their child was:
121. Hannah Rowe,⁵ b. ———, 18—. d. infant.

37. Ezra Steiner[4] m. Mary Fogler in ———, 1813 (?). She was born ———, and died June 9, 1874. He lived in Frederick.

Their children were:
122. Margaret Elizabeth Steiner,[5] b. Dec. 25, 1814 (300).
123. Elizabeth Steiner,[5] b. Feb. 10, 1817. d. young.
124. William Steiner,[5] b. Feb. 18, 1818 (305).
125. Charity Steiner,[5] b. Dec. 11, 1822. Single. d. ———.
126. Mary Ann Cecilia Steiner,[5] b. Feb. 21, 1824 (309).

38. Henry[4] Steiner m. Susan Haller on Apr. 15, 1812. She was born Jan. 17, 1790, and died Mch. 13, 1865. He was superintendent of the Alms House of Frederick County in 1837, was a farmer in Mount Pleasant, Woodsboro' and Middletown, and died in Frederick City.

Their children were:
127. William Henry Steiner,[5] b. June 26, 1813. d. July 15, 1816.
128. David Christian Steiner,[5] b. Aug. 19, 1814 (317). d. Feb. 16, 1892.
129. John Alexander Steiner,[5] b. Mch. 16, 1816 (324).
130. Denton Lloyd Steiner,[5] b. Nov. 17, 1817. Single. d. Aug. 8, 1835.
131. Jacob Frederick Steiner,[5] b. Jan. 4, 1821 (333). d. Oct. 24, 1876.
132. Daniel Nicholas Steiner,[5] b. Oct. 16, 1822. d. Feb. 29, 1824.
133. Henry Christopher Steiner,[5] b. Mch. 12, 1824 (343). d. Aug. 12, 1863.
134. Barbara Ann Elizabeth Steiner,[5] b. May 14, 1826. d. July 22, 1827.
135. Herman Francis Steiner,[5] b. Mch. 25, 1830 (349).
136. Susan Rebecca Steiner,[5] b. Jan. 9, 1833 (362).

41. Jacob Steiner[4] m. Elizabeth Lotta on ———, 1820. She was born ——— and died Nov. 8, 1829. He was a carpenter, lived in Frederick, and died when 26 years old.

Their child was:
137. Elizabeth Steiner, b. July 23, 1821. Single. d. Mch. 25, 1868.
In the latter part of her life this most estimable lady resided with the family of Dr. Lewis H. Steiner.

42. Christian[4] Steiner married his second cousin Rebecca Weltzheimer on Dec. 7, 1823. Mrs. Steiner was born on April 20, 1802, and died April 21, 1862. She was the elder of the two daughters of Dr. Lewis Weltzheimer, of Frederick City, and Margaret Meyer, of Sheverstadt, near Frederick. Margaret Meyer was born Oct. 15, 1772, and baptized Feb. 28, 1773, and was the daughter of Christopher Meyer and

THE GENEALOGY OF THE STEINER FAMILY. 37

Anna Margaret Ramsburg, the daughter of Stephen. Christopher Meyer was confirmed in the Reformed Church in 1754, and bought the estate of Sheverstadt from Elias Brunner, his wife's uncle, in 1771. The farm is still in the possession of the family, being owned by the estate of the late Lewis H. Steiner. Christopher Meyer's mother's name was Anna Barbara. She died in 1789. He was often known as "Stoffel." His father was Caspar Myer, who bought part of Tasker's Chance from Daniel Dulany on July 28, 1746, and sold land in Frederick County on Feb. 3, 1759 (Liber F, 641). He died in 1773. Lewis Weltzheimer was the son of John Philip Weltzheimer and Maria Magdalena Straszer, and was born July 16, 1769, at Pirmasens, now a part of Rhenish Bavaria; but, at that time, a part of the possessions of Hesse Darmstadt. From that early home in the Vosges of the Palatinate, he emigrated to America with his brother Philip, who settled in Shepherdstown, W. Va. On May 5, 1796, Lewis Weltzheimer opened the first apothecary's store in Fredericktown. His advertisement in Bartgis's Federal Gazette reads as follows: "Fresh Drugs and Medicines. Lewis Weltzheimer Informs the public in general and his friends in particular that he has just opened a New Medicinal Store next door to Mr. Francis Kleinerd's, at the sign of the Golden Mortar in Fredericktown, near the gaol, where he intends to sell and will be constantly supplied with a general assortment of genuine Drugs and Medicines, together with all sorts of Painter's Colours and Paints." Dr. Weltzheimer was an educated man. At the baptism of his daughter Rebecca, the sponsors were John Jacob Rohr and his wife Catharine. There was a second daughter, Caroline, born July 16, 1807, who married Adam Wolfe. Lewis Weltzheimer died Dec. 10, 1834.

Christian Steiner was one of a large family and early had to start in business for himself. He was for some time clerk in a store at Mechanicstown (now Thurmont). Later he removed to Frederick, married, and in ———, 1824, at the age of twenty-seven, opened a general store on Market Street, just above Fourth Street. He was a uniformly successful merchant, respected by all men for his probity and uprightness of character. His rule of life may well be summed up in a sentence from a letter to his son, on May 10, 1854: "When I commenced the world, I resolved (as I was poor and success depended upon an upright course) that I never would do an unworthy act knowingly." Having amassed a modest competence, he sold out his business to Joshua Doub and Joseph G. Miller for $6114 on Sept. 21, 1842. He then retired from active business and spent his time in caring for his property and in the conduct of various institutions in which he was interested. He was long a director in the Fredericktown Savings Institution, and was one of the founders and first trustees of the Frederick Female Seminary. He was a consistent member of the Evangelical Reformed Church of Frederick, in which he was confirmed in 1821 and in whose service he several

38   THE GENEALOGY OF THE STEINER FAMILY.

times held the office of elder. In politics he was an ardent Whig. His kindness and thoughtfulness towards his wife, who was an invalid during the latter years of her life, are worthy of special mention.

Children of Christian Steiner and Rebecca Weltzheimer:
138. Matilda Margaret[5] Steiner, b. Sept. 5, 1824. d. June 16, 1826.
139. Lewis Henry[5] Steiner, b. May 4, 1827 (371). d. Feb. 18, 1892.
140. Ann Rebecca Louisa[5] Steiner, b. Feb. 28, 1829 (377). d. Jan. 8, 1896.
141. Elmira Elizabeth[5] Steiner, b. Apr. 14, 1833. d. July 24, 1834.

47. Elizabeth Wisenall[4] m. George Fayman (b. Feb. 28, 1790, d. ———), of Shepherdstown, W. Va. They had no children.

48. Catharine Wisenall[4] m. George Needy, of Shepherdstown, W. Va. They had no children.

50. John Wisenall[4] m. Ellen Rudy on Sept. 25, 1832 (b. July 17, 1813, and d. Dec. 12, 1893). He removed from Shepherdstown, W. Va., to Maysville, Ky., and after his death his widow removed to Aberdeen, Ohio. He was a carpenter.

Their children were:
142. John Bernard Wisenall,[5] b. July 2, 1833 (381).
143. Josephine Wisenall,[5] b. July 27, 1839. Unmarried. Lives at Aberdeen, Ohio.
144. Mary Catharine Wisenall,[5] b. Mch. 12, 1842. Unmarried. Lives at Aberdeen, Ohio.

52. Charlotte Steiner[4] m. Lewis Ramsburgh, of Frederick City, Md., on May 1, 1821. They had no children.

53. Daniel Steiner[4] m. widow Julia A. (Birely) Larkin on Sept. 27, 1832. He lived at Cumberland, Md.

Their children were:
145. Son.
146. Son.

54. Col. Frederick B. Steiner[4] m. Catharine Munder (b. ———, d. Feb. 22, 1876) on May 14, 1850. He was engaged in the business of importing fruit, in the firm of Dix & Steiner, at Baltimore, for many years. He now resides on his farm in Anne Arundel County in summer and in Baltimore in the winter.

Their children were:
147. Charles Steiner, b. Oct. 24, 1854. Single. d. Aug. 16, 1876.

THE GENEALOGY OF THE STEINER FAMILY.

148. Emma Steiner, b. Feb. 26, 1856. Musical directress. Lives in New York City.

55. Catharine⁴ Derr m. Jacob Reese, farmer and magistrate, of Frederick City, on June 6, 1822 (he was b. Dec. 9, 1791, and d. ———, 1872). They had no children.

56. John Derr⁴ m. Elizabeth Lugenbeel (b. Jan. 13, 1808, d. Aug. 3, 1883) on Apr. 8, 1830. He was a farmer, residing on his place, Dearbought, near the original estate of Jacob Steiner. For many years he was director of the Farmers' and Mechanics' Bank of Frederick. His wife was the great-grand-daughter of Elizabeth Keyser, of Germantown, Pa., and of the family of Leonard Keyser, of Bavaria, who was burned for his religious opinions in 1527.

Their children were:
149. Catharine E. Derr,⁵ b. Aug. 18, 1831. d. Apr. 13, 1840.
150. Margaret Ann Derr,⁵ b. Dec. 4, 1832 (388). d. Jan. 21, 1862.
151. Mary Louisa Derr,⁵ b. Mch. 7, 1834. Unmarried.
152. John Peter Derr,⁵ b. Oct. 30, 1835 (389). d. Dec. 20, 1869.
153. Thomas Melanchthon Derr,⁵ b. Oct. 20, 1837. Unmarried. Sailed Oct. 1860 as supercargo from New York of brig Bahia, laden with merchandise for Dominican Government. d. Dec. 3, 1860, of yellow fever at Port au Prince on return from St. Domingo.
154. W. H. Derr,⁵ b. Oct. 2, 1839. d. Dec. 22, 1839.
155. Son,⁵ b. Feb., 1841. d. Mch., 1841.
156. Alice Virginia Derr,⁵ b. Feb. 24, 1842. Unmarried.
157. Eugene Lugenbeel Derr,⁵ b. Feb. 7, 1844 (389).
158. William Reese Derr,⁵ b. July 23, 1846 (389).
159. Charles Worman Derr,⁵ b. Feb. 16, 1849. Unmarried. Lawyer. d. Aug. 9, 1883.
160. Ezra Zacharias Derr,⁵ b. Jan. 12, 1852 (391).

57. Elizabeth Derr m. Jonathan Getzendanner, farmer, of Frederick County (b. Mch. 19, 1798, d. Jan. 8, 1859), on Apr. 12, 1821.

Their children were:
161. Catharine Elizabeth Getzendanner,⁵ b. ———, 182— (393). d. Jan. 26, 1884.
162. John Derr Getzendanner,⁵ b. Apr. 25, 1823 (402). d. Feb. 17, 1879.
163. William Abraham Getzendanner,⁵ b. Jan. 12, 1825. Single. d. Aug. 15, 1846.
164. Mary Ann Getzendanner,⁵ b. ———, 182— (404). d. ———, 18—.
165. Ann Rebecca Getzendanner,⁵ b. Oct., 1829 (?) (410). d. Aug. 5, 1880.

166. Lewis Getzendanner,⁵ b. Feb. 17, 1830. Single. In Walker's Nicaragua expedition, he died about 1856.
167. Jacob Reese Getzendanner,⁵ b. July 26, 1832 (414).
168. Thomas Getzendanner,⁵ b. ———, 183— (416).

58. Mary Derr⁴ m. Daniel Getzendanner, bro. Jonathan (b. ———, d. ———, 1873) on Dec. 21, 1823. They lived in Frederick.

Their children were:
169. Edward Tabler Getzendanner,⁵ b. Jan. 22, 1825 (421).
170. Elizabeth Catharine Getzendanner,⁵ b. June, 1827. Single. d. Sept. 12, 1846.
171. Daniel Getzendanner,⁵ b. Sept. 26, 1829 (428).
172. Anna Mary Getzendanner,⁵ b. June 4, 1831 (435).
173. John Augustus Getzendanner,⁵ b. Sept. 23, 1833 (441).
174. Francis Marion Getzendanner,⁵ b. June 30, 1835 (443).
175. George Washington Getzendanner,⁵ b. May 13, 1837 (443).
176. Martha Victoria Getzendanner, b. Jan. 29, 1839 (649). d. ———, 1878.
177. Harrison Getzendanner,⁵ b. Oct. 6, 1840 (451).
178. Calvin Rose Getzendanner,⁵ b. Aug. 16, 1842. Single. d. Nov. 10, 1870.
179. Milton Eugene Getzendanner,⁵ b. Jan. 23, 1845 (452).

61. Maria Steiner⁴ m. Nicholas Lease.
180.

65. Jonathan Steiner⁴ m. Sally Barnhart on Mch. 21, 1837. He lived in Winchester, Va., and later (in 1858) in Alexandria, Va. He was a carpenter.

Their children were:
181-1. George F. Steiner,⁵ b. ———, 18— (459).
181-2. James Steiner,⁵ b. ———.
181-3. Ettie Steiner,⁵ b. ———.
181-4. Mary Steiner,⁵ b. ———.
181-5. Sallie Steiner,⁵ b. ———.

66. Rev. Jesse Steiner⁴ m. ¹ Sarah Catharine Leighou on Dec. 8, 1839 (b. ———, 18—, d. at Yellow Springs, Greene Co., Ohio, Nov. 4, 1876); ² Mary E. Norman, on June 6, 1877 (b. ———, 18—). He was confirmed in the Frederick Reformed Church. by Rev. J. H. Schmaltz in 1832, and that year entered the Reformed High School at York, Pa. After studying there and at the Reformed Theological Seminary, and

graduating from the latter June, 1837, he preached near Trenton, N. J., as a licentiate for a year. In 1838 he was ordained by Susquehanna Classis of the Reformed Church and placed in charge of three congregations in Northumberland Co., Penn. He preached there until 1841. From then to 1843 he had no charge. In 1844 he removed to Ohio and became pastor of seven congregations at and near Lancaster in that State. In 1846 he removed to the Fairfield charge, composed of four congregations, in the Miami classis, and in 1852 to Union charge of four congregations in the same classis, living in Springfield, Ohio. In 1856 he became pastor of the Congregational Church at Peoria, Ill., in the Illinois Central Association. In 1858 he returned to Maryland and lived at Walkersville, Frederick County, in charge of the Glade Church. This charge he retained until 1867, when he accepted a call to the Taneytown charge in Carroll County, Md. In 1872 he returned to Ohio and, settling at Ashland, served the Shenandoah charge of five congregations in the Tuscarawas classis. This church he left in 1875 to become pastor of the St. Paul's charge of three congregations in the Miami classis in Champaign Co., Ohio. In 1877 he removed to Greenville, Ohio, and had charge of the New Madison Church. Two years later he settled without charge on a farm two miles from Millerstown, Champaign Co., Ohio. In 1882 he returned to the ministry and took the Bunker Hill charge of three congregations in Williams Co., Ohio, residing at Pulaski. In 1885 he again retired from active service and spent his remaining years on his farm near Millerstown. He was an active and zealous man, positive and decided in his views, and a fluent and forceful speaker, rarely using notes. He favored emotional religion, had a strong and vivid imagination, was a clear thinker, a logical reasoner and a ready debater, being well versed in parliamentary law. He told his friend Rev. I. H. Reiter: " If you ever write my biography say Jesse Steiner was a radical." The friend adds: " He was a man of strong intellectual endowments, had a penetrating mind, was quick of perception and creditably educated . . . and well versed in the Holy Scriptures and the general doctrines of the church."

Children of Jesse and S. C. (Leighou) Steiner:
182. Laura Steiner,[5] b. ———, 1842. d. young.
183. Florence Gertrude Steiner,[5] b. ———, 1843 (460).
184. Oscar Steiner,[5] b. ———, 1847 (463). d. Dec. 11, 1883.
185. Alice J. Steiner,[5] b. ———, 1849 (464).

Children of Jesse and M. E. (Norman) Steiner:
186. Norman Steiner,[5] b. ———, 187—.
187. Jesse Steiner,[5] b. ———.

67. Ann Elizabeth Steiner[4] m. [1] Joseph Neal, a tinner, of Cumberland, Md., on Nov. 19, 1839; [2] John T. Kitto.

188. John Neal,[6] b. ———. Living in Baltimore.

68. Joshua [4] Steiner m. Catharine Wickard, ———, 184—, who is still living. He lived at Cumberland, Md. He was a carpenter and builder. He was a devout member of the Methodist Episcopal Church.

Their children were:
189-1. John W. Steiner,[5] b. Aug. 10, 1843 (467-1).
189-2. Mary Margaretta Steiner,[5] b. Oct. 24, 1845 (467-5). d. ——, 18—.
189-3. Ann Eliza Steiner,[5] b. Feb. 20, 1848 (467-6).
189-4. Laura Lavinia Steiner,[5] b. Oct. 22, 1850 (467-10).
189-5. Kate O. Reese Steiner,[5] b. Aug. 22, 1853 (467-11).
189-6. Florence Arabella Steiner,[5] b. May 23, 1857 (467-14).
189-7. Charles A. Seay Steiner,[5] b. June 11, 1860 (467-17).

72. William Ramsburg [4] m. Diana Neese (b. Jan. 29, 1822, d. Dec. 21, 1853). He removed to West Milton, Miami Co., Ohio.

Their child was:
190. John Thomas Ramsburg,[5] b. Dec. 20, 1853. d. Aug. 26, 1854.

73. Mary Ramsburg [4] m. John Fredk. Wm. Hanshew (b. Feb. 19, 1790, d. May 6, 1867).

Their child was:
191. Henry E. Hanshew,[5] b. Nov. 11, 1824 (468).

74. Catharine Ramsburg [4] m. Geo. Enos on Dec. 10, 1829. They had no children.

75. Sophia Ramsburg [4] m. Arnold S. Stonebraker (b. Mch. 6, 1811), Nov. 1, 1832.

Their children were:
192. William T. Stonebraker,[5] b. July 4, 1834 (473).
193. Charles R. Stonebraker,[5] b. Nov. 14, 1836 (474).
194. Minerva J. Stonebraker,[5] b. May 5, 1847 (478).

77. Susanna Ramsburg [4] m. George Seibert, of Urbana, Ohio (b. May 3, 1817, d. July 8, 1848), on Aug. 23, 1838.

Their children were:
195. Frances Seibert,[5] b. Sept. 2, 1840 (479).
196. Catharine Elizabeth Seibert,[5] b. July 6, 1842.
197. George Todd Seibert,[5] b. July 20, 1848.

THE GENEALOGY OF THE STEINER FAMILY. 43

78. Daniel T. Ramsburg[4] m. Mary Elizabeth Young (b. May 12, 1819) on Apr. 15, 1856. He lived at Poolesville, Montgomery Co., Md.
Their children were:
198. William Thomas Ramsburg,[5] b. Mch. 17, 1857.
199. Samuel Young Ramsburg,[5] b. July 23, 1858.
200. Clara Ramsburg,[5] b. June 30, 1864.
201. Daniel Stephen Ramsburg,[5] b. Nov. 2, 1866.
202. George Brewer Ramsburg,[5] b. Mch. 27, 1867.

80. George W. Stoner[4] m. Ann Elizabeth Bowlus (b. Mch. 12, 1800, d. aged about 73). He lived at Westerville, O., and was a farmer. He was married May 6, 1824.
Their children were:
203. John W. Stoner,[5] b. Jan. 26, 1825. d. Oct. 7, 1837.
204. Ann Rebecca Stoner,[5] b. Mch. 5, 1826. d. Nov. 1, 1842.
204-1. Ann Sophia Stoner,[5] b. Mch. 6, 1827 (479-1). d. Oct. 31, 1849.
204-2. William H. Stoner,[5] b. Feb. 23, 1828. d. Sept. 29, 1848.
204-3. Ann Elizabeth Stoner,[5] b. Jan. 10, 1830 (479-3). d. Jan. 30, 1895.
204-4. Ann Marie Stoner,[5] b. Dec. 22, 1832 (479-7). d. July 15, 1851.
204-5. Milton Stoner,[5] b. July 11, 1834 (479-13).
204-6. George W. Stoner,[5] b. Aug. 15, 1837 (479-16).
204-7. Charlotte Stoner,[5] b. Dec. 11, 1841 (479-16).

81. John Stoner[4] m. Mch. 5, 1822, in Frederick County, Md., Elizabeth Baltzell (b. Dec. 13, 1802, d. Dec. 23, 1843). He was a farmer, and removed to Ohio in 1822. After John Stoner's death, his widow married David Risden, by whom she had children.
Their children were:
205. George Washington Stoner,[5] b. Apr. 18, 1823 (479-24). d. Aug. 27, 1883.
205-1. Susanna M. Stoner,[5] b. Mch. 5, 1825 (479-25). d. Aug. 6, 1847.
206. John Eli Stoner,[5] b. Apr. 15, 1827 (479-26).

84. Christian C. Stoner[4] m. Ann Maria Smith on May 19, 1831 (she was b. Aug. 16, 1812, and d. Dec. 3, 1852). He was a farmer.
Their children were:
207. Charles A. Stoner,[5] b. Mch. 13, 1833 (479-27).
208. Samuel H. Stoner,[5] b. Aug. 10, 1834 (479-28). d. Jan. 23, 1892.
208-1. John S. Stoner,[5] b. Feb. 28, 1837. d. Nov. 8, 1864.
209 Richard S. Stoner,[5] b. ———, 1838 (479-32).
209-1. Henrietta V. Stoner,[5] b. Feb. 15, 1839 (479-35).

210. Marietta F. Stoner,⁵ b. Feb. 3, 1842 (479-38).
210-1. Theodore Stoner,⁵ b. ———, 1843 (479-39). d. Feb., 1871.
210-2. Ellen A. Stoner, ⁵ b. ———, 1844 (479-40).
210-3. Otterbein Stoner,⁵ b. ———, 1845. d. infant.
210-4. Calvin Stoner,⁵ b. ———, 1845. d. infant.
210-5. Jesse H. R. Stoner,⁵ b. Mch. 14, 1847. Cincinnati, Ohio.
210-6. Anna Stoner,⁵ b. ———, 1849. d. infant.
210-7. Alive B. Stoner,⁵ b. June 16, 1851 (479-42).

Christian C. Stoner m. ² Sarah Dick (b. ———, 1830, d. Aug. 1874) in Sept., 1853.

Their children were:
210-8. Blanche A. Stoner,⁵ b. June 26, 1854. d. Mch., 1871.
210-9. Edgar C. Stoner,⁵ b. June, 1856. Clerk, Kansas City, Mo.
210-10. Eva K. Stoner,⁵ b. Jan. 16, 1858 (479-42).
210-11. Cora O. Stoner,⁵ b. Jan., 1860 (479-42).
210-12. George B. Stoner,⁵ b. Apr., 1862 (479-43).
210-13. Joseph H. Stoner,⁵ b. Aug. 6, 1864. Merchant, Kansas City, Mo.

85. Susan Stoner⁴ m. John Fout (b. Sept. 17, 1802, d. Sept. 1, 1884) on Jan. 13, 1835.

Their child is:
211. Ann Rebecca Fout,⁵ b. Sept. 10, 1836.

87. Ann E. Stoner⁴ m. James Durbin on Nov. 29, 1831.

Their child was:
212. Edward Durbin, b. ———, 1840. d. about 1868.

89. Dennis C. Stoner⁴ m. Charlotte Smith on Jan. 16, 1838. He was a farmer, living near Tiffin, O. She was b. July 1, 1815, d. Jan. 26, 1853.

Their children were:
213. John Alexander Stoner,⁵ b. Oct. 7, 1838 (480).
213-1. Winfield Scott Stoner,⁵ b. Aug. 2, 1840. d. July 28, 1848.
214. Francis Edwin Stoner,⁵ b. Apr. 15, 1842 (480-3). d. Aug. 9, 1885.
215. Henry Stoner,⁵ b. Apr. 1, 1844. Farmer, Tiffin, Ohio. d. Jan. 24, 1879.
216. Laura Victoria Stoner,⁵ b. June 11, 1847. d. Mch. 4, 1872.
216-1. Charlotte E. Stoner,⁵ b. Feb. 2, 1849. d. Apr. 4, 1869.
216-2. Thomas C. Stoner,⁵ b. Oct. 27, 1850 (480-5).
216-3. Susannah Stoner,⁵ b. Jan. 1853. d. June, 1855.

Dennis C. Stoner m. ² Marion O. Dick, Sept., 1853 (she was b. Nov. 25, 1834, and d. Oct. 5, 1891).

THE GENEALOGY OF THE STEINER FAMILY. 45

Their children were:
216-4. Dow S. Stoner,⁵ b. July, 1854. d. Jan., 1855.
216-5. Willia R. Stoner,⁵ b. Jan., 1856 (480-9).
216-6. Jessie W. Stoner,⁵ b. Feb. 16, 1857. d. Mch. 2, 1861.
216-7. Nellie H. Stoner,⁵ b. Oct. 12, 1859. d. Sept. 11, 1875.
216-8. Douglas A. Stoner,⁵ b. Dec., 1861 (480-11). d. Mch. 29, 1895.
216-9. Fannie K. Stoner,⁵ b. Apr., 1863. d. ———.
216-10. Ada M. Stoner,⁵ b. Jan., 1866 (480-11).
216-11. Oakley D. Stoner,⁵ b. ———, 186—. d. Aug. 18, 1866.
216-12. Maud O. Stoner,⁵ b. Jan., 1869. Lives at Tiffin.
216-13. Florence B. Stoner,⁵ b. June, 1870. Lives at Tiffin. Teacher.
216-14. Ralph Stoner,⁵ b. Sept., 1873. Lives at Tiffin. Clerk.

92. Lewis B. Eader,⁴ of Frederick City, Md., married on May 6, 1824, Catharine Brengle (b. ———, d. Feb. 18, 1890).

Their children were:
217. Eliza Catharine Eader,⁵ b. Aug. 15, 1825 (481).
218. David Nicholas Eader,⁵ b. Oct. 2, 1827 (481). d. Oct. 5, 1882.
219. Jonathan Eader,⁵ b. Dec. 7, 1829 (483). d. May, 1894.
220. Anna Mary Eader,⁵ b. Mch. 17, 1832 (484). d. Aug. 29, 1876.
221. Charles Ezra Eader,⁵ b. Aug. 10, 1834 (484). d. July 3, 1863.
222. William Henry Eader,⁵ b. June 9, 1837 (488). d. Nov. 23, 1883.
223. Rachel Louisa Eader,⁵ b. July 27, 1839.
224. Daniel Root Eader,⁵ b. Jan. 18, 1842 (494).
225. Peter Mantz Eader,⁵ b. July 16, 1844 (496).

95. Elizabeth Derr⁴ m. John Maule, of Frederick, Md., farmer (b. ———, 1792, d. ———, 1865), on ———, 18—.

Their children were:
226. Llewellah Thomas Maule,⁵ b. Feb. 19, 1829 (500).
227. Ann Elizabeth Maule,⁵ b. Mch. 23, 1830 (501). d. Feb. 25, 1881.
228. William Wesley Maule,⁵ b. Dec. 11, 1832 (506).
229. Lydia Margaret Maule,⁵ b. Mch. 18, 1833 (514).
230. Charles Lewis Maule,⁵ b. Jan. 9, 1835 (514). d. Mch. 23, 1865.
231. John Ezra Maule,⁵ b. ———, 1839. d. young.

96. Ezra Derr⁴ m. Rosanna Cramer, Jan., 1832. He was a farmer and lived in ———, Ohio.

Their children were:
232. John Thomas Derr,⁵ b. Nov. 17, 1832 (517).
233. Belinda Catharine Derr,⁵ b. Apr. 11, 1834 (519). d. June 7, 1865, from fall from a chair.

46   THE GENEALOGY OF THE STEINER FAMILY.

 234. Dennis Frederick Derr,⁵ b. May 17, 1836 (523).
 235. Mary Margaret Derr,⁵ b. July 22, 1838. d. Sept. 1, 1861.
 236. William Derr,⁵ b. May 31, 1842 (526).
 237. David Henry Derr,⁵ b. May 5, 1844 (526).
 238. Clarinda Ann Derr,⁵ b. Aug. 25, 1847. Single. Lives on old homestead.

 97. Margaret Derr⁴ m. Wm. Baker, of Dayton, Ohio, on Nov. 18, 1832.

Their children were:
 239. Elinore Baker,⁵ b. Sept. 24, 1833. d. June 17, 1834.
 240. Susan Emily Baker,⁵ b. Mch. 25, 1835 (528).
 241. Anne Elizabeth Baker,⁵ b. Sept. 22, 1838 (533).
 242. John Wesley Baker,⁵ b. Sept. 26, 1840 (537).
 243. William Henry Baker,⁵ b. Dec. 18, 1843 (542).
 244. Mary Isabelle Baker,⁵ b. Sept. 24, 1847 (545).
 245. Alice Sophia Baker,⁵ b. Sept. 14, 1849 (552).

 100. James O. Steiner,⁴ farmer, of Buckeystown, Frederick Co., m. on Jan. 27, 1869, Marietta Roderick.

Their child is:
 246. Rodney Benedict Steiner,⁵ b. Dec. 8, 1869.

 101. Wm. R. Steiner,⁴ dealer in fertilizers, Frederick City, m. Feb. 12, 1873, Amanda Jane Yarborough (b. Raleigh, N. C., Oct. 18, 1842).

Their child is:
 247. Daisy Yarborough Steiner,⁵ b. Dec. 4, 1878, in Frederick City.

 104. Anna S. Hauser⁴ m. ——— Winecaff (b. ———, d. ———).

Their children were:
 248. Charles Winecaff,⁵ b. ———, 18— (556).
 249. William Winecaff,⁵ b. ———, 18—. d. killed on railroad.
 250. Emma Winecaff,⁵ b. ———, 18— (557).
 251. Anna Winecaff,⁵ b. ———, 18— (558).

 106. Almedia S. Hauser⁴ m. ——— Hoye, of Garrett Co., Md.

Their children were:
 252. Adolphus C. Hoye,⁵ b. ———, 1877. d. ———, 1880, aet. 3 yrs. 10 mos.
 253. Marion S. Hoye,⁵ b. ———. Unmarried.

THE GENEALOGY OF THE STEINER FAMILY. 47

107. Margaret E. Stoner⁵ m. ¹Dr. Chas. Klotz (b. in Dusseldorf, Prussia, d. May 22, 1872) on Apr. 15, 1841; ²Michael Edie Hess, Justice of the Peace, on Sept. 18, 1878. She lives at Edenburg, Knox township, Clarion Co., Penn., and has had no children.

108. Susannah Stoner⁵ m. on May 21, 1850, James M. Fackender, of Sligo, Clarion Co., Penn., a farmer (b. Feb. 19, 1825).

Their children are:
254. Ann Stoner Fackender,⁶ b. Mch. 22, 1852 (559).
255. Victoria A. Fackender,⁶ b. Aug. 8, 1854 (559).
256. Ella Fackender,⁶ b. Nov. 2, 1856. d. Nov. 17, 1856.
257. George Washington Fackender,⁶ b. Oct. 21, 1858 (563). d. Mch. 30, 1893.

109. John W. Stoner,⁵ of Oil City, Venango Co., Pa., farmer, m. ¹May 24, 1859, Sarah Ann Russell. He was divorced from her in 1876, and m. ²Jane Best (b. ———, 1836) in 18—.

Children of J. W. and S. A. (Russell) Stoner:
258. Charles Flavius Stoner,⁶ b. June 15, 1860 (568).
259. Elriporter Stoner,⁶ b. July, 1861. d. Aug., 1862.
260. William Parker Stoner,⁶ b. May 5, 1866. Keeps a store at Oil City.
261. Ida M. Stoner,⁶ b. May 21, 1868. d. ———, 1870.
262. John A. Stoner,⁶ b. Apr. 4, 1872. d. Jan. 31, 1873.

110. Caroline Stoner,⁵ of Sligo, Clarion Co., Pa., m. ¹Josiah Paine (b. Aug. 5, 1819, d. ———), contractor, on Oct. 21, 1858; ²and William Graham (b. ———, 1819, d. Aug. 1, 1864); and ³John Dilley (farmer) on Aug. 24, 1873.

Child of Josiah and Caroline (Stoner) Paine:
263. Margaret Anne Paine,⁶ b. Apr. 11, 1860. d. ———, 1862.

Child of Wm. and Caroline (Stoner) Graham:
264. Donna Rosa Graham,⁶ b. Apr. 30, 1864. d. Oct. 5, 1864.

111. Hannah M. Stoner⁵ m. Jan. 5, 1865, Wm. Thompson (b. July 16, 1827), of Curllsville, Clarion Co., Pa. He has been an oil operator, storekeeper and farmer, and while serving three years in the Civil War was twice wounded.

Their children were:
265. Lucy May Thompson,⁶ b. Feb. 25, 1866 (571).
266. Ida Stoner Thompson,⁶ b. Oct. 8, 1868. d. summer of 1894.

112. Thomas S. Stoner,[5] farmer, of Sligo, Clarion Co., Pa., m. on Mch. 18, 1856, Narcissa Craig (b. Feb. 23, 1836).

Their children were:
267. David Stoner,[6] b. Nov. 21, 1856. d. Dec. 4, 1860.
268. Anna L. Stoner,[6] b. Sept. 15, 1858 (573).
269. Hannah Margaret Stoner,[6] b. Mch. 10, 1861 (577).
270. Ambrose E. B. Stoner,[6] b. Nov. 20, 1863. d. Dec. 4, 1864.
271. Charles S. Stoner,[6] b. Oct. 3, 1867.
272. R. G. Stoner,[6] b. Jan. 22, 1870 (578).
273. Della B. Stoner,[6] b. Mch. 23, 1873.

113. Heiner A. Stoner,[5] farmer, of Toby Township, Clarion Co., Pa., m.[1] on Feb. 22, 1859, Margaret Jane Rankin (b. June 15, 1841, in Toby Township, d. Oct. 27, 1861);[2] Ann Bole (b. June 11, 1843) on July 31, 1862.

Child of H. A. and M. J. (Rankin) Stoner:
274. David Stoner,[6] b. Dec. 26, 1860 (579).

Children of H. A. and Ann (Bole) Stoner:
275. Flora Lily Stoner,[6] b. Mch. 10, 1864 (583).
276. Flavius Josephus Stoner,[6] b. Apr. 10, 1870.
277. John Hurlbert Stoner,[6] b. May 8, 1873.

115. Elizabeth Stoner[5] m. David W. Herstine, of Pittsburg, Pa., on June 9, 1853. He was b. June 24, 1825; d. Feb. 16, 1875.

Their children were:
278. May Herstine,[6] b. Apr. 29, 1854. d. May 3, 1854.
279. Solomon Stoner Herstine,[6] b. June 13, 1855. d. Sept. 30, 1889.

116. Catharine W. Stoner[5] m. Dr. Thos. W. Shaw (b. Jan. 25, 1826) on Mch. 14, 1854. They live in Pittsburg, Pa.

Their children were:
280. Henry Clay Shaw,[6] b. Feb. 26, 1855 (586).
281. Charles Stoner Shaw,[6] b. Sept. 13, 1856. M. D.
282. Margaret Wolfe Shaw,[6] b. July 29, 1858 (588).
283. George Elmer Shaw,[6] Apr. 3, 1861. Attorney-at-law.
284. Catharine Emily Shaw,[6] b. Dec. 3, 1863. d. Feb. 6, 1892.
285. Thomas Wilson Shaw,[6] b. Dec. 27, 1867.
286. Howard Shaw,[6] b. July 10, 1872.
287. Elizabeth Shaw,[6] b. Nov. 3, 1876.
288. Woodward Scott Shaw,[6] b. Aug. 25, 1880.

THE GENEALOGY OF THE STEINER FAMILY. 49

117. J. Madison Stoner[5] m. Aurelia Eliza Palmer (b. Sept. 29, 1839), of Stonington, on Aug. 16, 1859. He is an attorney-at-law and, with the exception of a few years spent in California, has lived in Pittsburg, Pa.

Their children were:
289. Mary Margaret Stoner,[6] b. May 23, 1860.
290. Frank Rahm Stoner,[6] b. Aug. 13, 1862 (588).
291. Aurelia Eliza Stoner,[6] b. Oct. 17, 1865.
292. James Madison Stoner,[6] b. Mch. 20, 1868.
293. Edmund Curtis Stoner,[6] b. Jan. 13, 1871.
294. Eva Stoner,[6] b. Apr. 29, 1873.
295. William Wirt Stoner,[6] b. Mch. 11, 1875.
296. Marcus Woodward Stoner,[6] b. June 3, 1878.

118. Victoria Stoner[5] m. Rev. Jno. J. Murray, D. D., of the Methodist Protestant Church, on Nov. 29, 1877. They now reside at Union Bridge, Carroll Co., Md. They have no children.

119. Alfred M. Stoner[5] m. Sept. 1, 1870, widow Catharine (Hollins) Allen (b. ———, 1847).

Their child is:
297. Katharine Stoner,[6] b. June 22, 1871 (588).

120. Anna M. Stoner[5] m. Oct. 10, 1866, Marcus A. Woodward (b. Mch. 28, 1836), attorney-at-law, of Pittsburg, Pa.

Their children were:
298. Anna Woodward,[6] b. Jan. 26, 1868.
299. Marcus Woodward,[6] b. Oct. 31, 1882.

122. Margaret E. Steiner[5] m. July 14, 1839, W. Conrad, of Frederick City (b. ———, d. ———, 18—).

Their children are:
300. Ezra Conrad,[6] b. ———, 184—. d. young.
301. Henrietta Conrad,[6] b. ———, 18—. d. young.
302. Fannie Conrad,[6] b. ——— (589).
303. Joseph Conrad,[6] b. ———.
304. Ann Cadelia Conrad,[6] b. ——— (592).

124. William Steiner[5] m. Eva Stockman.

Their children were:
305. Melissa Virginia Steiner,[6] b. ———, 18— (593).

306. Sophia Steiner,⁶ b. ——, 18— (594).
307. Anna Mary Steiner,⁶ b. ——, 18— (595).
308. Alice Steiner,⁶ b. ——, 18— (597).

126. Mary A. C. Steiner⁵ m. Enos Clemm, of Walkersville, Frederick Co., Md.

Their children were:
309. Anna Mary Clemm,⁶ b. ——.
310. Laura Virginia Clemm,⁶ b. ——.
311. Jeannette Clemm,⁶ b. ——.
312. Della Clemm,⁶ b. ——.
313. Emma Henrietta Clemm,⁶ b. ——.
314. Julia Clemm,⁶ b. ——.
315. Charles McClellan Clemm,⁶ b. ——.
316. Eugene Augustus Clemm,⁶ b. ——.

128. Captain David C. Steiner m. Mch. 18, 1838, Elizabeth Wiest. He was a butcher by trade, and later a greengrocer. He enlisted as first lieutenant in the First Maryland Cavalry at the opening of the Civil War, and was promoted to the position of quartermaster, serving in that capacity with Slocum's corps at Vicksburg and Gettysburg. After the war he lived in West Virginia, at Glens Falls, N. Y., and Baltimore, where he died.

Their children were:
317. Charles Reighley Steiner,⁶ b. Nov. 22, 1838. d. Apr. 15, 1839.
318. Denton Wiest Steiner,⁶ b. May 22, 1840. d. Nov. 8, 1847.
319. Valetta Steiner,⁶ b. Jan. 10, 1842 (598).
320. Alice Steiner,⁶ b. Mch. 22, 1845 (603).
321. Jacob Henry Steiner,⁶ b. Nov. 14, 1847. d. Nov. 15, 1847.
322. Grace Fetterhafen Steiner,⁶ b. Jan. 18, 1853 (322).
323. Mary Elizabeth Steiner,⁶ b. July 9, 1855.

129. Gen. John A. Steiner⁵ m. ¹ Sophia Myers (b. Mch. 27, 1819; d. Aug. 26, 1842) on Apr. 13, 1837; ² on Sept. 19, 1844, Mary Ann Brunner (b. Feb. 9, 1823; d. Mch. 8, 1894). He received his education at the Frederick Academy (now Frederick College) and private schools in Frederick City and County. He learned the trade of boot and shoe making, and followed the trade for a number of years. Then he engaged in the lumber and brick business, during which time he was appointed clerk to the County Commissioners for Frederick County, organizing the office, it being then separated from the office of the Clerk of the Circuit Court of the county. He was for several terms elected as one of the Board of Common Council, a part of the corporate authorities of Fred-

erick City. In early life he became a member of the Evangelical Reformed Church of Frederick, where he was engaged as teacher, manager, and superintendent of the Sunday school for more than sixty years, and very frequently was elected by the congregation as deacon and elder. He was often delegate to classis and synods of that denomination and was elected vice-president of the Synod of the Potomac at its session held at Carlisle, Pennsylvania, in 1890. When the rebellion of the Southern States occurred, he volunteered and entered the service as the major of the 1st Regiment Potomac Home Brigade Volunteers; was promoted to the lieutenant-colonelcy, and was honorably discharged, upon resignation, June, 1863, just before the enemy crossed the Potomac River into Maryland. He refused to receive his discharge until the enemy was driven from the State, volunteered and with his regiment fought through the battle of Gettysburg, Pennsylvania, where the regiment was attached to 12th (Slocum's) Corps and Lockwood's Maryland Brigade. The history of the war records the service of the brigade at several most important points during the engagements of the battle. After the enemy was defeated and driven into Virginia, he accepted his discharge and returned to his family in Frederick. For this volunteer service, the Senate of the United States breveted him to a full colonelcy and brevet brigadier-general U. S. volunteers. At the fall election of 1863, he was elected sheriff of Frederick County, which office he filled during its term of two years. At the election of 1866, he was elected as one of the delegates from Frederick County to General Assembly of Maryland, and there served on several important committees, among which was the committee on claims and corporations. Upon his return from Annapolis, after serving in the House of Delegates, he resumed the manufacture of brick, later retiring from that business he returned to his former trade, boot and shoe making. In July, 1882, he received from Col. E. H. Webster, collector of customs for the port of Baltimore, an appointment of day inspector of customs, and as such served until 1888, mainly as chief of debenture department. After Mr. Cleveland reached the presidency of the United States, he was retired to make place for a democrat. Shortly after his return home, Dr. George Diehl purchased the "Examiner" printing office and selected him as his office editor, in which capacity he served until advancing age forced him to retire to private life. General Steiner was connected with a number of organizations. For more than fifty years he was a member of the Junior Steam Engine Company No. 1 of Frederick, and served as a director and vice-president in the company. He was connected with Columbia Lodge, F. and A. M., Odd Fellows, Improved Order of Red Men, Knights of Pythias, and for many years was a director in the Young Men's Bible Society of Frederick County. By his zeal and willing service he usually became prominent in the organizations to which he was attached.

THE GENEALOGY OF THE STEINER FAMILY.

Children of Jno. A. and Sophia (Myers) Steiner:
324. Calvin Myers Steiner,[6] b. Feb. 20, 1839. d. Nov. 30, 1851.
325. Susan Sophia Steiner,[6] b. Nov. 22, 1841 (605). d. ———, 18—.

Children of Jno. A. and Mary A. (Brunner) Steiner:
326. Charles Henry Steiner,[6] b. July 8, 1845 (607).
327. Mary Amelia Steiner,[6] b. Nov. 13, 1848. d. Nov. 28, 1851.
328. John Edgar Steiner,[6] b. Oct. 6, 1851. d. Nov. 28, 1851.
329. Ira Frank Steiner,[6] b. Nov. 2, 1852 (607).
330. Kate Brunner Steiner,[6] b. Jan. 9, 1856.
331. Fannie Elizabeth Steiner,[6] b. Feb. 4, 1858 (608).
332. Edward Everett Steiner,[6] b. July 26, 1860. Agent Ætna Insurance Co., Baltimore.

131. Jacob F. Steiner[5] m. Mch. 2, 1843, Sophia Cramer (b. Sept. 12, 1821). He lived at Fostoria, Seneca Co., Ohio.

Their children were:
333. Emma Jane Steiner,[6] b. Apr. 7, 1844.
334. Mary Ellen Steiner,[6] b. July 15, 1846. d. Nov. 1, 1852.
335. Annette Catharine Steiner,[6] b. Mch. 28, 1849. d. Sept. 7, 1852.
336. Luther Edward Steiner,[6] b. Sept. 9, 1851. d. Feb. 9, 1858.
337. Susan Laura Steiner,[6] b. Dec. 29, 1853. d. Mch. 18, 1880.
338. Millard Francis Steiner,[6] b. July 10, 1856 (608).
339. Jacob Henry Steiner,[6] b. Nov. 29, 1858. d. Mch. 21, 1859.
340. Carrie Elizabeth Steiner,[6] b. Jan. 9, 1860 (612).
341. Virginia Steiner,[6] b. Nov. 14, 1862. d. Jan. 2, 1869.
342. Hepron Cramer Steiner,[6] b. Aug. 4, 1866.

133. Henry C. Steiner[5] m. Feb. 3, 1848, Ann Elizabeth Rohr (b. May 26, 1819). He lived in Frederick City.

Their children are:
343. Clara Hauer Steiner,[6] b. Nov. 12, 1848. Teacher in Samuel Ready School, Baltimore.
344. William Chapin Steiner,[6] b. July 2, 1850 (614).
345. Henry Rohr Steiner,[6] b. Feb. 20, 1852. Apothecary, Frederick City.
346. Louisa Hart Steiner,[6] b. Mch. 16, 1854.
347. Susan Steiner,[6] b. May 22, 1856.
348. Daniel Hicks Steiner,[6] b. Apr. 26, 1861. Apothecary, Frederick City.

135. H. Francis Steiner[5] m. Apr. 9, 1856, Othella Jane Fout (b. June 23, 1835), daughter of Otho and Catharine (Crum) Fout.

THE GENEALOGY OF THE STEINER FAMILY. 53

Their children were:
349. Lilian Catharine Steiner,⁶ b. Apr. 6, 1857 (616).
350. Henry Otho Steiner,⁶ b. June 19, 1858. d. Nov. 18, 1863.
351. Francis Marion Steiner,⁶ b. Oct. 4, 1859 (619).
352. John William Steiner,⁶ b. Nov. 1, 1860. d. Nov. 9, 1860.
353. Orlean May Steiner,⁶ b. Nov. 13, 1861 (622).
354. Gracy Steiner,⁶ b. Feb. 4, 1864 (623).
355. Bertha Virginia Steiner,⁶ b. Nov. 25, 1865.
356. Harry Stair Steiner,⁶ b. Dec. 1, 1867. d. Aug. 3, 1868.
357. Ann Rebecca Steiner,⁶ b. June 16, 1869.
358. David Steiner,⁶ b. Feb. 28, 1872 (624).
359. Mary Rose Steiner,⁶ b. Sept. 1, 1874.
360. George Steiner,⁶ b. July 31, 1876. d. Aug. 6, 1889.
361. Roland Steiner,⁶ b. June 27, 1880.

136. Susan R. Steiner⁵ m. Mch. 23, 1853, Ethan Allen Cramer, of Frederick City (b. Apr. 29, 1830).

Their children were:
362. Denton William Cramer,⁶ b. Feb. 14, 1854. d. Oct. 15, 1856.
363. Ida Virginia Cramer,⁶ b. Nov. 20, 1855 (624). d. June 4, 1891.
364. Cora May Cramer,⁶ b. Oct. 6, 1857 (624).
365. Joseph Carty Cramer,⁶ b. Dec. 29, 1859 (631).
366. Willie McClellan Cramer,⁶ b. Nov. 13, 1861. d. Jan. 4, 1881.
367. Susan Phoebe Cramer,⁶ b. Dec. 22, 1863.
368. Eli Henry Cramer,⁶ b. May 17, 1866 (636).
369. Edward Allen Cramer,⁶ b. Nov. 15, 1870 (636).
370. Charles Francis Cramer,⁶ b. Mch. 25, 1872 (638).

139. Lewis H. Steiner⁵ m. Oct. 30, 1866, Sarah Spencer Smyth, of Guilford, Conn.

Their children are:
371. Bernard Christian Steiner,⁶ b. Aug. 13, 1867, Librarian of the Enoch Pratt Free Library of Baltimore City, Associate in History at the Johns Hopkins University, A. B. Yale, 1888, A. M. Yale, 1890, Ph. D. J. H. U., 1891, LL. B. Univ. of Md., 1894. Instructor in History in charge of that department at Williams College, 1891-92.
372. Gertrude Rachel Steiner,⁶ b. Aug. 21, 1869.
373. Walter Ralph Steiner,⁶ b. Nov. 18, 1870. A. B. Yale, 1892. Student at the Johns Hopkins University 1892 to date.
374. Bertha Rebecca Steiner,⁶ b. July 6, 1872.
375. Ralph Dunning Smyth Steiner,⁶ b. Sept. 11, 1874. d. Feb. 18, 1877.
376. Amy Louise Steiner,⁶ b. June 16, 1877.

THE GENEALOGY OF THE STEINER FAMILY.

Lewis H. Steiner was fitted for college at the Frederick Academy, whence he entered the Sophomore class of Marshall College, at which institution he was graduated in 1846. During his college course he was much influenced by his contact with such professors as J. W. Nevin, D. D., Philip Schaff, D. D., and Traill Green, M. D. He then pursued the study of medicine in the office of a Frederick physician and at the Medical Department of the University of Pennsylvania, where he received the degree of M. D. in 1849. In the same year Marshall College gave him the degree of A. M. in course. He received the same degree (honoris causa) from the College of St. James in 1854 and from Yale College in 1869.

He began the practice of medicine in Frederick, but in 1852 removed to Baltimore to assist Dr. John R. W. Dunbar in the conduct of a private medical institute. He continued in that position until 1855. His attention was early directed to natural science, particularly to botany and chemistry, and he soon gave up the active practice of medicine to devote his time to teaching these sciences. He was one of the earliest physiological chemists in the country, and his monograph on strychnia is well known. From 1853 to 1856 he was professor of chemistry and natural history at the Columbian University, as well as professor of chemistry and pharmacy and dean of the National Medical College. He was lecturer on chemistry and physics at the College of St. James from 1854 to 1859. In 1855 and 1856 he was Swann lecturer on applied chemistry in the Maryland Institute, and in the latter year was one of those who reorganized the Maryland College of Pharmacy, in which institution he served as professor of chemistry until 1861. During this period he also lectured on chemistry and botany in many private schools for girls in and near Baltimore. In particular, he was one of the corporators of and professors in the Mt. Washington Female College. He was Librarian of the Maryland Historical Society from 1856 to 1861. At the outbreak of the Civil War Dr. Steiner returned to Frederick and entered the U. S. Sanitary Commission as one of its inspectors. In 1863 he was promoted to the position of Chief Inspector for the Army of the Potomac and placed in full charge of the field relief work. In recognition of his valuable services in the war, the New York Commandery of the Military Order of the Loyal Legion of the United States elected him a companion of the third class in 1868.

In 1865 he was chosen President of the School Board of Frederick County, and acting as such until 1868, he thoroughly organized the school system of that county. In 1871 he was elected, on the Republican ticket, as the member from Frederick County of the State Senate, in which body he was for a session the only representative of his party. He was re-elected in 1875 and 1879, but defeated in 1883. While in that body he was usually a member of the committee on rules, on engrossed bills, and other important committees. In-1876 he was a member of the

THE GENEALOGY OF THE STEINER FAMILY. 55

National Republican Convention, which nominated Gen. R. B. Hayes to the presidency. From 1873 until 1884, he was political editor of the Frederick Examiner.

In November, 1884, he was chosen Librarian of the Enoch Pratt Free Library of Baltimore City. He organized the library, which was opened at the beginning of 1886, with 20,000 volumes and a central and four branch libraries. A fifth branch library was opened in 1888, and the books owned by the library were over 100,000 at Dr. Steiner's death in 1892. Under Dr. Steiner's administration, the library circulated about 450,000 books annually among the people of Baltimore.

In 1853 he was chosen a Fellow of the Medical and Chirurgical Faculty of Maryland; in 1853 Member and in 1874 Fellow of the American Association for the Advancement of Science; in 1852, Member of the American Medical Association; in 1855, Correspondent of the Philadelphia Academy of Natural Science; in 1869, Corresponding Member of the Maryland Academy of Sciences; in 1872, Member and in 1876 Vice-President of the American Public Health Association; in 1876, Corresponding Member of the New Haven Colony Historical Society; in 1878, Trustee of the Hampton Normal and Agricultural Institute; in 1891, Vice-President of the American Library Association; in 1856, he was made an honorary member of the Alpha of New York of the Φ B K Fraternity; in 1853, a member of the Maryland Historical Society; in 1876, a member of the International Medical Congress in Philadelphia; and in 1881, Corresponding Member of the New England Historic Genealogical Society. In 1876 he was one of the founders of the American Academy of Medicine, of which he was vice-president in 1876 and 1877 and president in 1878. In 1886 he was one of the original members of the Society for the History of the Germans in Maryland. He was assistant editor of the American Medical Monthly from 1858 to 1861.

He received the degree of LL. D. from Delaware College in 1884, and that of Litt. D. in 1887 from Franklin and Marshall, at which time he delivered the oration at the celebration of the centennial of the founding of the college.

His first publication was an address delivered in 1851 before the Goethean Literary Society of Marshall College, of which he was a member. He translated Wills' "Chemical Analysis" with Dr. D. Breed in 1854, and between 1865 and 1880 translated nearly a dozen works of German fiction for the Reformed Church Publication House. He contributed numerous monographs and reviews to medical and scientific journals, and published many addresses, and scientific and other reports.

In 1876 he edited the History of Guilford, Connecticut, left in manuscript by his father-in-law, the Hon. R. D. Smyth, and in 1889 he acted as one of the Committee of Arrangements for the Quarto Millennial Celebration of the settlement of that town.

He was a prominent member of the Reformed Church in the United

56   THE GENEALOGY OF THE STEINER FAMILY.

States, and served several times as elder in the Evangelical Reformed Church at Frederick and as treasurer of the Potomac Synod. In 1863 he was one of the secretaries of the Tercentenary Celebration of the Heidelberg Catechism; in 1866, a member of the committee to prepare an "Order of Worship" for the church; in 1874, a member of a committee to prepare a "Hymn Book"; from 1878 to 1883, a member of the Peace Commission, and a member of a committee to prepare a "Directory of Worship" in 1883. Together with Prof. Henry Schwing, he prepared two hymn books: "Cantate Domino" in 1859 and "Tunes for Worship" in 1884.

140. Ann Rebecca L. Steiner[5] m. Mch. 18, 1847, Fairfax Schley, M. D., of Frederick City.

Their children are:
377. Rebecca Maria Schley,[6] b. Dec. 2, 1847. d. Jan. 2, 1848.
378. Steiner Schley,[6] b. Apr. 24, 1849 (639).
379. Jennie Schley,[6] b. Feb. 24, 1851 (643).
380. Lewis Henry Schley,[6] b. Dec. 19, 1854. A. B. Franklin and Marshall, 1875. d. June 12, 1877.
381. Agnes Schley,[6] b. July 27, 1857.

142. John B. Wisenall m. May 20, 1867, Jane E. Campbell, of Aberdeen, Ohio (b. June 1, 1840). He was a carpenter at Maysville, Ky., for a number of years. In 1876 he removed to Covington, Ky., and has now retired from business.

Their children are:
382. Paul (Dimmitt) Wisenall,[6] b. Mch. 29, 1868. Inland Oil Company, Cincinnati, Ohio.
382-1. Bernard Thompson Wisenall,[6] b. Sept. 4, 1869. Architect, 75 Blymyer Building, 216 Main St., Cincinnati, O.
383. Grace Bierbower Wisenall,[6] b. July 28, 1871. Teacher.
384. Christian Steiner Wisenall,[6] b. Feb. 20, 1873. Book-keeper, Anderson, Ind.
385. John Wisenall,[6] b. Feb. 11, 1875. drowned Aug. 29, 1882.
386. Elinor Jane Wisenall,[6] b. Oct. 11, 1876.
387. Daniel Church Wisenall,[6] b. Feb. 3, 1883.

150. Margaret A. Derr[5] m. Apr. 27, 1858, Edward Shriner, miller, of Ceresville, Frederick, Co.

Their child is:
388. Edward Derr Shriner,[6] b. Jan. 13, 1862 (643).

THE GENEALOGY OF THE STEINER FAMILY. 57

152. John P. Derr[5] m. Ann C. N. Warner, of Baltimore (b. Sept. 6, 1836; d. Aug. 30, 1890), on Oct. 4, 1859. Prior to the Civil War he conducted the largest cotton trade in Baltimore and was the first to secure through transit for cotton from the South to that city. He then returned to Frederick County, settled at Ceresville, and in 1867 became president of the Frederick and Liberty Turnpike Co., of which he was chief promoter. He was killed by the bursting of a mill-dam. They had no children.

157. Eugene L. Derr[5] m. Mch. 20, 1876, Frances Groverman (b. Feb. 9, 1844; d. Nov. 1, 1886). They had no children. He is a farmer and occupies the old homestead at Ceresville, Frederick Co. He has been president of the Frederick County Agricultural Society and of the Board of County Commissioners.

158. William R. Derr[5] m. Nov. 9, 1869, Fannie Brengle Gittinger (b. Aug. 11, 1847). He is a merchant in Baltimore.

Their children are:
389. Frances Elizabeth Derr,[6] b. Apr. 14, 1872.
390. Willie May Derr,[6] b. July 30, 1876.

160. Ezra Z. Derr,[5] M. D., m. Jan. 29, 1880, Julia Latham, of New Brunswick, N. J. He is surgeon in the U. S. Navy, having entered the service in 18—. He was on the U. S. S. Nipsic at Samoa at the time of the terrible hurricane of March 16, 1889, and by conducting a free hospital for the natives on the island, received the warmest testimonials from King Malietoa and the London Missionary Society, as well as kind recognition from the U. S. Naval Department. Under the pseudonym of A. Z. Rred, he published a work entitled "Evolution versus Involution," a popular exposition of the doctrine of true evolution, a refutation of the theories of Herbert Spencer and a vindication of theism. This has been reviewed very favorably.

Their children are:
391. John Sebastian Derr,[6] b. Jan. 6, 1881.
392. Kate Norman Derr,[6] b. Mch. 12, 1886.

161. Catharine E. Getzendanner[5] m. Oct. 27, 1842, Henry Leiter, of Champaign, Ill (b. ———, 18—; d. Jan. 18, 1868).

Their children were:
393. Frances Leiter,[6] b. Sept. 25, 1844 (643). d. ———, 18—.
394. Edward Thomas Leiter,[6] b. July 13, 1846 (644).
395. Mary Jane Leiter,[6] b. Sept. 7, 1848. d. ———, 18—.
396. Lewis Henry Leiter,[6] b. Sept. 20, 1850 (645).

58   THE GENEALOGY OF THE STEINER FAMILY.

397. John William Leiter,⁶ b. Feb. 24. 1852 (646). d. ———, 18—.
398. Alice V. Leiter,⁶ b. July 25, 1855.
399. Rolla Morgan Leiter,⁶ b. Mch. 16. 1858.
400. Charles Eugene Leiter,⁶ b. Oct. 23, 1860 (647).
401. Elmer Grant Leiter,⁶ b. Oct. 7. 1864.

162. John D. Getzendanner⁵ m. Charlotte E. Pettengall (b. Mch. 20, 1826) on Apr. —, 1845. He was a merchant in Frederick City and a farmer in Frederick County.

Their children are:
402. John William Getzendanner⁶ b. ———. 1846 (648).
403. Samuel Pettengall Getzendanner,⁶ b. May 14. 1848. d. ———, 18—.

164. Mary A. Getzendanner⁵ m. Nov., 1845. John Bechtol (b. ———. d. ———), a dentist. They lived in Texas.

Their children were:
404. Scott Bechtol,⁶ b. ———, 18—. Dentist. Lives in Texas.
405. Lewis Bechtol,⁶ b. ———. 18—. Dentist. Lives in Texas.
406. David Bechtol,⁶ b. ———. 18—. Farmer. Lives in Texas.
407. Gilla Bechtol,⁶ b.———. 18—. d. ———, 18—.
408. Mollie Bechtol,⁶ b. ———. 18— (652).
409. Fannie Bechtol,⁶ b. ———. 18— (653).

165. Ann R. Getzendanner⁵ m. Wm. H. Hughes. in the B. & O. R. R. office (b. Mch. 10, 1814; d. Dec. 19. 1874).

Their children are:
410. Elizabeth F. Hughes,⁶ b. Oct. 20. 1852 (654).
411. Wendell Hughes,⁶ b. Nov. 26. 1854 (657). d. Jan. 26. 1893.
412. William Samuel Hughes,⁶ b. Nov. 26. 1854 (660).
413. Florence Patterson Hughes,⁶ b. May 6. 1866 (665).

167. Jacob R. Getzendanner⁵ m. Ann V. Fleming. daughter Joseph, on Mch. 14. 1854.

Their children are:
414. Virginia Getzendanner,⁶ b. Jan. 21. 1855 (666).
415. Elizabeth Getzendanner,⁶ b. ———. 18—.

168. Thomas Getzendanner⁵ m. ¹Anna Mary Wilcoxon and ²Mary Carlin.

THE GENEALOGY OF THE STEINER FAMILY. 59

Children of Thomas and A. M. (Wilcoxon) Getzendanner:
416. Florence Getzendanner,⁶ b. ———, 18— (668).
417. Estelle Getzendanner,⁶ b. ———, 18— (669).
418. Minnie Getzendanner,⁶ b. ———, 18— (670).

Children of Thomas and Mary (Carlin) Getzendanner:
419. Winfield Getzendanner,⁶ b. ———, 18—.
420. Jennie Getzendanner,⁶ b. ———, 18—.

169. Edward F. Getzendanner⁵ m. ¹———, 18—, Catharine E. Schaeffer (b. Oct. 10, 1831; d. May 31, 1871); ² Verlinda C. Young (b. Aug. 21, 1831). He is a farmer in Montgomery Co., Md.

By his first wife he had:
421. Anna Mary Getzendanner,⁶ b. May 23, 1849. d. July 10, 1864.
422. Laura Virginia Getzendanner,⁶ b. Aug. 15, 1850 (671).
423. Winton E. Getzendanner,⁶ b. Sept. 20, 1852 (671).
424. Daniel J. Getzendanner,⁶ b. Jan. 8, 1855 (671).
425. William R. Getzendanner,⁶ b. Feb. 24, 1858 (672).
426. Addie E. Getzendanner,⁶ b. May 1, 1861 (673).
427. Nannie May Getzendanner,⁶ b. May 28, 1867 (643).

171. Daniel Getzendanner⁵ m. Margaret E. Winebrenner (b. Jan. 26, 1837) on Dec. 12, 1854, formerly a merchant, he is now a farmer in Jefferson Co., W. Va. He has been nominated by the Republican party of his county for sheriff and twice for State Senator.

Their children are:
428. Charles Christian Getzendanner,⁶ b. Dec. 2, 1855 (675).
429. Clara Catharine Getzendanner,⁶ b. Dec. 14, 1857 (675).
430. Henry Clay Getzendanner,⁶ b. Jan. 14, 1861 (679).
431. Louis David Getzendanner,⁶ b. Dec. 27, 1862. Hardware merchant, Charlestown, W. Va.
432. Phoebe E. Getzendanner,⁶ b. June 21, 1867.
433. Franklin Getzendanner,⁶ b. Sept. 23, 1868. In Treasury Department at Washington.
434. Mary Getzendanner,⁶ b. June 2, 1873.

172. Anna Mary Getzendanner⁵ m. Andrew Jackson Wilcoxon (b. May 11, 1829) on Apr. 15, 1851. He is a lumber merchant at Frederick City.

Their children are:
435. Daniel Clinton Wilcoxon,⁶ b. Aug. 6, 1852 (654).
436. William Wilcoxon,⁶ b. Jan. 22, 1854 (681).

437. Francis M. Wilcoxon,[6] b. Nov. 21, 1858. Merchant, Baltimore.
438. Clara Wilcoxon,[6] b. Mch. 12, 1863 (686).
439. Harry J. Wilcoxon,[6] b. Jan. 1, 1869. d. Apr. 22, 1877.
440. George Wilcoxon,[6] b. Mch. 9, 1871. Ironfounder, Frederick.

173. John A. Getzendanner,[5] of Fort Worth, Texas, m. ———, 1864, Margaret Martin.

Their children are:
441. Bernard Getzendanner,[6] b. ———, 18—. Cashier in bank at Fort Worth.
442. Lelia Getzendanner,[6] b. ——— (689).

174. Francis M. Getzendanner[5] m. Sarah E. Young, ———, 18— (b. June 17, 1843). He is a farmer in Montgomery Co., Md. They have no children.

175. George W. Getzendanner,[5] farmer, lives in Nebraska. He m. Catharine Prattsman (b. ———, d. ———).

Their children are:
443. Arthur Getzendanner,[6] b. ———, 18—. d. ———, 1880.
444. Minnie Getzendanner,[6] b. ———, 1866 (   ).
445. George H. Getzendanner,[6] b. ———, 1868.
446. Catharine Getzendanner,[6] b. ———.
447. Lillian Getzendanner,[6] b. ———.
448. Elizabeth P. Getzendanner,[6] b. ———.
449. Katie Getzendanner,[6] b. ———.
450. Eddie Getzendanner,[6] b. ———, 18—. d. ———, 1880.

177. Rev. Harrison Getzendanner,[5] a clergyman of the Reformed Church, resides in Missouri. He m. Fannie Myers on ———, 18—.

Their child is:
451. Eugene Getzendanner,[6] b. ———, 18—.

179. Milton E. Getzendanner,[5] merchant, of Frederick City, m. Dec. 12, 1867, Clara Virginia Smith.

Their children are:
452. Mary Frank Getzendanner,[6] b. Jan. 18, 1872. d. Sept. 8, 1872.
453. Katie Eugenia Getzendanner,[6] b. Jan. 20, 1873 (691).
454. Nellie Clara Getzendanner,[6] b. July 24, 1875.
455. Bessie May Getzendanner,[6] b. May 20, 1879.
456. Emma Grace Getzendanner,[6] b. July 16, 1880.

THE GENEALOGY OF THE STEINER FAMILY.

457. Clara Gertrude Getzendanner,⁶ b. May 23, 1883.
458. Susan Nixdorff Getzendanner,⁶ b. Aug. 13, 1885.

181. George F. Steiner⁵ m. Amanda M. Sinn on Apr. 2, 1861.
Their child was:
459. Henrietta Virginia Steiner,⁶ b. Mch. 28, 1862.

183. Florence G. Steiner⁵ m. ———, 1863, David M. Scholl, merchant, of Frederick City.

Their children are:
460. Lilly May Scholl,⁶ b. ———, 1864 (692).
461. Harry Steiner Scholl,⁶ b. ———, 1867. d. ——— 4, 1869.
462. Frank Scholl,⁶ b. ———, 1872.

184. Oscar Steiner⁵ m. Fannie Haugh.
Their child was:
463. George Lewis Steiner,⁶ b. ———.

185. Alice J. Steiner⁵ m. J. J. Ashenhurst, of Canton, Ohio, on ———.

Their children are:
464. Harry Ashenhurst,⁶ b. ———.
465. Florence Gertrude Ashenhurst,⁶ b. ———.
466. Alice Ashenhurst,⁶ b. ———.

189-1. John W. Steiner⁵ m. Alice G. Malone, May 18, 1881. He is a printer.

Their children are:
467-1. Grace G. Steiner,⁶ b. June 26, 1882.
467-2. Laura C. Steiner,⁶ b. June 24, 1885. d. Aug. 25, 1887.
467-3. Ruth E. Steiner,⁶ b. Oct. 25, 1891. d. Jan. 2, 1893.
467-4. Florence Esther Steiner,⁶ b. May 9, 1895.

189-2. Mary M. Steiner⁵ m. A. F. Brennan, of Lonaconing, Md.

Their child is:
467-5. Oscar Brennan,⁶ b. about 1870. In marine service, Washington, D. C.

189-3. Ann E. Steiner⁵ m. Henry J. Fredericks, Jan. 5, 1870.

THE GENEALOGY OF THE STEINER FAMILY.

Their children are:
467-6. Mary M. Fredericks,⁶ b. Sept. 2, 1872.
467-7. William Harrison Fredericks,⁶ b. Oct. 9, 1874.
467-8. Kate Naomi Fredericks,⁶ b. Oct. 15, 1876.
467-9. Frank Alfred Fredericks,⁶ b. Dec. 30, 1878.

189-4. Laura L. Steiner⁵ m. James M. Kegg, Aug. 17, 1875. Live at Bedford, Pa.

Their child is:
467-10. Horace Virgil Kegg,⁶ b. Aug. 31, 1877.

189-5. Kate O. R. Steiner⁵ m. James W. Shuck, Jan. 12, 1875. They live at Allegheny City, Penn.

Their children are:
467-11. William C. Shuck,⁶ b. in Baltimore, May 11, 1876.
467-12. Edgar A. Shuck,⁶ b. in Cumberland, June 23, 1882.
467-13. Kate L. Shuck,⁶ b. in Cumberland, Oct. 16, 1890. d. Bedford, Pa., Aug. 16, 1891.

189. Florence A. Steiner⁵ m. Thomas A. Learned on Oct. 30, 1878.

Their children are:
467-14. Ralph Benson Learned,⁶ b. Dec. 26, 1879.
467-15. Thomas Alvin Learned,⁶ b. June 3, 1882.
467-16. Carl Leon Learned,⁶ b. Dec. 3, 1884.

189-7. Charles A. S. Steiner⁵ m. Annie E. Taafel, Nov. 27, 1884. He is in the employ of the West Virginia Central Railroad at Cumberland, Md.

Their children are:
467-17. Eda S. Steiner,⁶ b. Sept. 16, 1885. d. Dec. 15, 1893.
467-18. May K. Steiner,⁶ b. Dec. 24, 1887.
467-19. Lucy T. Steiner,⁶ b. Jan. 24, 1890. d. Mch. 20, 1894.

191. Henry E. Hanshew⁵ m. ¹ Mch. 24, 1846, Caroline M. Keller (b. Aug. 2, 1820; d. Apr. 28, 1868); ² Mary E. Marriott, of Georgetown, D. C., on Sept. 24, 1872. He lives at Germantown, Montgomery Co., Md.

Children of H. E. and C. M. (Keller) Hanshew:
468. John Keller Hanshew,⁶ b. Jan. 5, 1847. d. ———.
469. Charles Frederick Hanshew,⁶ b. Mch. 17, 1848.
470. Mary Catharine Hanshew,⁶ b. June 14, 1851.

THE GENEALOGY OF THE STEINER FAMILY. 63

471. Caroline Virginia Hanshew,[6] b. Dec. 25, 1855.
472. Henry Muhlenberg Hanshew,[6] b. Jan. 31, 1859. d. Nov. 13, 1862.

192. Wm. T. Stonebraker[5] m. Emma Belle (b. Sept. 16, 1849), May 16, 1867.
Their child is:
473. Horace Grant Stonebraker,[6] b. Sept. 29, 1868.

193. Chas. R. Stonebraker[5] m. Anna A. Coleman (b. Apr. 22, 1834) on Aug. 24, 1858.
Their children are:
474. George Wilbur Stonebraker,[6] b. Sept. 19, 1859.
475. Frances Minerva Stonebraker,[6] b. Apr. 24, 1862.
476. Clarence Elmer Stonebraker,[6] b. Feb. 3, 1865.

194. Minerva J. Stonebraker[5] m. John E. Mast (b. Sept. 12, 1838) on Apr. 13, 1869.
477.

195. Frances Seibert[5] m. John M. Carter (b. ———, 1822; d. Feb. 28, 1869) on Apr. 13, 1865.
Their child is:
479. George Seibert Carter,[6] b. Oct. 29, 1867.

204-1. Ann Sophia Stoner[5] m. Rev. John C. Bright (b. Oct. 13, 1818; d. Aug. 6, 1866) on Sept. 5, 1844.
Their children were:
479-1. George W. Bright,[6] b. Apr. 25, 1846 (694-1).
479-2. Mary E. Bright,[6] b. Sept. 18, 1847 (694-2).

204-3. Ann Elizabeth Stoner[5] m. [1]Jacob Souder (b. Apr. 20, 1825; d. Jan. 18, 1866) on Oct. 19, 1847; [2] Rev. W. B. Davis (b. ———; d. Jan. 30, 1895), Apr. 11, 1867. No children by the second marriage.
Children of Ann E. and Jacob Souder:
479-3. J. Winfield Souder,[6] b. July 28, 1849. d. Jan. 16, 1887.
479-4. Laura Belle Souder,[6] b. Feb. 7, 1852. New York. d. July 1, 1888.
479-5. Royal Edward Souder,[6] b. Nov. 26, 1857. d. Dec. 24, 1883.
479-6. William G. Souder,[6] b. Oct. 9, 1863 (694-8).

204-4. Ann Marie Stoner[5] m. her brother-in-law, Rev. John C. Bright, on July 15, 1851.

Their children were:

479-7. John L. Bright,[6] b. Dec. 5, 1852. Wholesale millinery merchant at Columbus, O.
479-8. Samuel E. S. Bright,[6] b. Dec. 23, 1854 (694-9). d. Oct. 13, 1880.
479-9. Anna A. Bright,[6] b. Dec. 31, 1856 (694-11).
479-10. Jesse Levi Bright,[6] b. May 28, 1859 (694-12).
479-11. Elsworth Bright,[6] b. Aug. 28, 1862 (694-14).
479-12. Jesse Cleone Bright,[6] b. Jan. 31, 1867. Westerville, Ohio.

204-5. Milton Stoner[5] m. Margaret Stoner on ———, 1852 (she was b. Feb., 1834). She claims to be a descendant of Benedict Stoner (4).

Their children were:

479-13. William F. Stoner,[6] b. May 25, 1856. Farmer, Tiffin, Ohio.
479-14. Cora V. Stoner,[6] b. May 1, 1858 (694-15).
479-15. Royal G. Stoner,[6] b. Oct., 1861. Tiffin, Ohio.

204-6. George W. Stoner[5] is a farmer at Kenton, Ohio. He married, Aug. 17, 1858, Jennie Souder (b. Mch. 30, 1840). They have no children.

204-7. Charlotte Stoner[5] m. Sept. 4, 1858, James Newcomb (b. Nov. 5, 1838), a salesman, at Westerville, Ohio.

Their children were:

479-16. Louis O. Newcomb,[6] b. Sept. 26, 1860. Railroadman.
479-17. Lillie D. Newcomb,[6] b. Mch. 2, 1862 (694-20).
479-18. Nellie E. Newcomb,[6] b. Jan. 28, 1864 (694-20).
479-19. Harry Newcomb,[6] b. Jan. 27, 1866. Salesman in millinery trade.
479-20. Fred. Newcomb,[6] b. Aug. 27, 1868 (694-22).
479-21. Martha Ellen Newcomb,[6] b. Feb. 28, 1877.
479-22. Jessie M. Newcomb,[6] b. May 1, 1879. d. Oct. 6, 1881.
479-23. Hattie M. Newcomb,[6] b. Nov. 25, 1883

205. George W. Stoner[5] m. Aug. 19, 1845, Hannah Cover (b. June 15, 1821), Gothenburg, Nebraska.

Their children were:

479-24. Mary Elizabeth Stoner,[6] b. May 30, 1846 (694-22-1).
479-24-1. Aaron E. Stoner,[6] b. Feb. 6, 1848 (694-22-5).
479-24-2. Martha Emily Stoner,[6] b. May 6, 1851. d. Aug. 26, 1852.
479-24-3. Anna Rebecca Stoner,[6] b. Mch. 8, 1854. d. Mch. 27, 1854.

THE GENEALOGY OF THE STEINER FAMILY.   65

479-24-4. Dennis Eli Stoner,⁶ b. Oct. 5, 1855. d. Oct. 26, 1855.
479-24-5. Alverda Leonora Stoner,⁶ b. Nov. 7, 1856 (694-22-5).
479-24-6. Adah Zillah Stoner,⁶ b. June 23, 1859 (694-22-9).
479-24-7. Emma Rosetta Stoner,⁶ b. Mch. 7, 1862 (694-22-11).

205-1. Susannah M. Stoner⁵ m. William Cromwell, a farmer, at Ladora, Henry Co., Ohio.
Their child is:
479-25. Mary Cromwell,⁶ b. July 21, 1846 (694-23).

206. John Eli Stoner⁵ m. Martha Ellen Rosenberger, May 18, 1847, and is a farmer at Marengo, Iowa.
Their children are:
479-26.   Catharine E. Stoner,⁶ b. June 29, 1849 (694-24).
479-26-1. Dennis L. Stoner,⁶ b. Jan. 22, 1855 (694-24).
479-26-2. Clara M. Stoner,⁶ b. Mch. 17, 1859 (694-24).
427-26-3. Almeda A. Stoner,⁶ b. Sept. 21, 1861 (694-24).
427-26-4. Theodore D. Stoner,⁶ b. Jan. 28, 1870 (694-24).
427-26-5. George N. Stoner,⁶ b. Sept. 5, 1873 (694-24).

207. Charles A. Stoner,⁵ merchant at Fremont, Ohio, m. Apr. 4, 1854, Catharine Zimmerman (b. in Md., Mch. 15, 1836).
Their children were:
479-27-1. Emma M. Stoner,⁶ b. Mch. 7, 1855. d. Sept. 12, 1856.
479-27-2. Anna M. Stoner,⁶ b. Apr. 10, 1857 (694-24).
479-27-3. Emmet C. Stoner,⁶ b. Mch. 14, 1859. d. Mch. 29, 1869.
479-27-4. Hallie A. Stoner,⁶ b. Jan. 14, 1867. d. Dec. 5, 1870.

208. Samuel H. Stoner,⁵ lumber dealer, Tiffin, Ohio, m. Sept. 27, 1870, Alice Baker, of Frederick, Md. (b. May 12, 1849).
Their children were:
479-28. Harry C. Stoner,⁶ b. Oct. 22, 1871. Clerk, B. & O. R. R. office, Tiffin, Ohio.
479-29. Glenna M. Stoner,⁶ b. Feb. 5, 1874. Tiffin.
479-30. Anna M. Stoner,⁶ b. June 30, 1876. Tiffin.
479-31. Mabel A. Stoner,⁶ b. Dec. 3, 1878. Tiffin.

209. Richard S. Stoner,⁵ commission merchant, Cincinnati, Ohio, m.

Their children were:

479-32. ———, b. ———. d. ———.
479-33. ———, b. ———. d. ———.
479-34. ———, b. ———. d. ———.

209-1. Henrietta V. Stoner[5] m. Oct. 25, 1860, John L. Oram (b. Feb. 16, 1835).

Their children were:
479-35. Orion Oram, b. ———, Dayton, Ohio.
479-36. Jessie Oram, b. ——— (694-25).
479-37. Glenna Oram, b. ——— (694-27).

210. Marietta F. Stoner[5] m. Dec. 23, 1879, Eugene W. Steenberg (b. Oct. 27, 1854).

Their child is:
479-38. Jesse Chatfield Steenberg,[6] b. Dec. 5, 1881.

210-1. Theodore Stoner[5] m. Mch. 22, 1866, Jennie Myers (b. May 5, 1845; d. Oct. 20, 1873). He was a farmer.

Their child is:
479-39. Frank Myers Stoner,[6] b. ———.

210-2. Ellen A. Stoner[5] m. ———.
479-40. } Boys, one named Chasey.
479-41. }

210-7. Alice B. Stoner[5] m. Rush Wolf, farmer, Rockaway, Ohio. No children.

210-10. Eva K. Stoner[5] m. May 27, 1890, George P. Cargill (b. ———; d. Jan. 6, 1896), of Kansas City. No children.

210-11. Cora O. Stoner[5] m. Jan. 10, 1882, John W. Frazee, of Kansas City.

Their child is:
479-42. Katie Marie Frazee,[6] b. Jan. 16, 1883.

210-12. George B. Stoner[5] m. Sept., 1892, Anna Thalheimer. He is a printer in Kansas City.
479-43.

THE GENEALOGY OF THE STEINER FAMILY. 67

213. Jno. A. Stoner⁵ m. Mch., 1862, Hetty A. Haines. He resides at Larned, Kansas, and is a dealer in groceries and queensware.

Their children are:
480. Raleigh G. Stoner,⁶ b. Apr., 1863. Jeweler, Larned, Kansas.
480-1. Jesse Lee Stoner,⁶ b. Apr., 1865 (695).
480-2. Mertie M. Stoner,⁶ b. Jan., 1867.

214. Francis E. Stoner,⁵ grocer, of Tiffin, Ohio, m. Apr. 17, 1872, Juliet O'Connor (b. Apr. 11, 1846).

Their children are:
480-3. Clark Stoner,⁶ b. Jan. 23, 1873. Grocer, Tiffin, Ohio.
480-4. Frances Edwin Stoner,⁶ b. Aug. 8, 1874. Grocer, Tiffin, Ohio.

216-2. Thomas C. Stoner,⁵ grocer, Tiffin, Ohio, m. Oct. 30, 1884, Fannie E. Rowland, of Baltimore, Md. (b. June 4, 1860).

Their children are:
480-5. Lee Rowland Stoner,⁶ b. Sept. 9, 1885.
480-6. Gertrude Marie Stoner,⁶ b. May 23, 1887. d. Oct. 11, 1894.
480-7. Helen Rebecca Stoner,⁶ b. Aug. 12, 1891.
480-8. Ruth Rowland Stoner,⁶ b. Mch. 16, 1894.

216-5. Willia R. Stoner⁵ m. William E. Dewald, of Tiffin, Ohio.

Their children are:
480-9. Chauncey Dewald,⁶ b. ———.
480-10. Paul Dewald,⁶ b. ———.

216-8. Douglas A. Stoner,⁵ carpenter, Tiffin, Ohio, m. Apr., 1884, Cora B. Keating (b. Feb. 9, 1863; d. Mch. 30, 1894). They had no children.

216-10. Ada M. Stoner⁵ m. Rev. Francis Shutly. They have no children.

217. Eliza C. Eader⁵ m. May 1, 1862, Wm. Henry Lewis. He is dead. They had no children.

218. D. Nicholas Eader⁵ m. Dec. 4, 1851, Margaret Duffie, of Frederick

Their children were:
481. Elizabeth Eader,⁶ b. ——— (696).
482. Ida Eader,⁶ b. ———. Single, living in Ohio.

68 THE GENEALOGY OF THE STEINER FAMILY.

219. Jonathan Eader⁵ m. Paulina Catharine Bridwell, May 4, 1852.

Their child was:
483. Lewis William Eader,⁶ b. ——— (697).

220. Anna M. Eader⁵ m. ———, 18—, Joseph Howell Talbott. They had no children.

221. Charles E. Eader⁵ m. July 27, 1857, Ann Catharine Lambright. He was killed at Gettysburg.

Their children were:
484. Rondo Chalmers Eader,⁶ b. ——— (son). d. young.
485. Ezra Clifton Eader,⁶ b. ———. d. ———, 1885.
486. Charles Elmer Eader,⁶ b. ——— (703).
487. Addie May Eader,⁶ b. ———. Single.

222. Wm. Henry Eader⁵ m. Dec. 6, 1860, Eliza Kelly. He lived in Tennessee and Colorado.

Their children were:
488. Joseph Eader,⁶ b. ———. d. young.
489. Charles Eader,⁶ b. ———.
490. Lewis Edmund Eader,⁶ b. ———.
491. Mary Eader,⁶ b. ———.
492. William Henry Eader,⁶ b. ———.
493. Walter Gregory Eader,⁶ b. ———.

224. Daniel R. Eader⁵ m. in Tennessee, ———, 18—, Annie ———. They have children.
494.

225. Peter M. Eader,⁵ blacksmith, of Frederick City, m. May 26, 1870, Sidney Ann Bruchey.

Their children are:
496. Walter Grason Eader,⁶ b. ———.
497. Bessie Olivia Eader,⁶ b. ———.
498. Pearl Alberta Eader,⁶ b. ———.
499. George Diehl Eader,⁶ b. ———.

226. Llewellah T. Maule⁵ m. Mary Masters, Nov., 1885. He is a farmer in Ohio.

Their child is:

THE GENEALOGY OF THE STEINER FAMILY. 69

500. Charles Llewellah Maule,⁶ b. May 11, 1877.

227. Ann E. Maule⁵ m. Adam Repp on ———, 1853.
Their children are:
501. Charles Wesley Repp,⁶ b. ———. Farmer, near Tiffin, Ohio.
502. Eliza Repp,⁶ b. ———. Single. d. aged 20.
503. Jesse Cyrus Repp,⁶ b. ———. Single. d. aged 22.
504. John Repp,⁶ b. ———. d. infant.
505. Laura Victoria Repp,⁶ b. ——— (705).

228. Wm. W. Maule⁵ m. ¹ Elizabeth Anne Belle, ———, 18—; ² Matilda C——— on ———, 18—. He is a farmer.
Children of W. W. and Elizabeth A. (Belle) Maule:
506. Lillie Maule,⁶ b. ———. d. young.
507. William Maule,⁶ b. ———. d. young.
508. Ada Maule,⁶ b. ——— (705).
509. Frank Maule,⁶ b. Apr. 30, 1866.
510. John Maule,⁶ b. Feb. 16, 1871.
511. Charles Henry Maule,⁶ b. ———. d. young.

Children of W. W. and Matilda (C———) Maule:
512. Jessie Maule,⁶ b. Jan., 1878.
513. Charles Maule,⁶ b. Mch. 3, 1881.

229. Lydia M. Maule⁵ m. Nov. 19, 1854, Wm. Dick (b. ———; d. ———, 1863). No children.

230. Chas. L. Maule⁵ m. Mary Jane Nichols, of Tiffin, Ohio, ———, 18—. He was in the Union army, and dying was buried in North Carolina.
Their children are:
514. Victoria Maule,⁶ b. ———, 1859 (708).
515. Laura Isabel Maule,⁶ b. ———, 1860 (710).
515. Didanna Ann Maule,⁶ b. ———, 1862 (711).
516. John Brough Maule,⁶ b. ⁶———, 1864 (711).

232. John T. Derr⁵ m. Minerva Shroyer, Oct. 6, 1857. He is a farmer in Ohio.
Their children are:
517. Ellen R. Derr,⁶ b. Sept. 18, 1858 (711).
518. William Addison Derr,⁶ b. Oct. 12, 1864 (715).

THE GENEALOGY OF THE STEINER FAMILY.

233. Belinda C. Derr[5] m. C. C. Park, Nov. 8, 1855.

Their children are:
519. Hiram G. Park,[6] b. Sept. 30, 1857 (716).
520. Ezra Derr Park,[6] b. Aug. 5, 1858. d. Mch. 4, 1871.
521. John C. Park,[6] b. Sept. 21, 1859 (717).
522. Anna Park,[6] b. Jan. 6, 1861 (718).
522-1. Henry Rockey Park,[6] b. Sept. 24, 1862. d. July 8, 1877.

234. Dennis F. Derr[5] m. Mary Jane Dudrow, Mch. ———, 1863. He is a farmer in Ohio.

Their children are:
523. Charles Ezra Derr,[6] b. Jan. 7, 1864 (720).
524. Annie Derr,[6] b. ———.
525. Minnie Derr,[6] b. ———.

236. Wm. Derr[5] m. Julia E. Miller, July 19, 1894. He is a farmer in Ohio.

237. David Hy. Derr[5] m. Mattie S. Kaga, Nov. 10, 1878. He is a farmer in Ohio.

Their children are:
526. Rosanna Blanche Derr,[6] b. Sept. 19, 1883.
527. Ezra C. Derr,[6] b. Oct. 26, 1885.

240. Susan E. Baker[5] m. Jan. 1, 1858, Julius Berkey, a large manufacturer, of Grand Rapids, Mich.

Their children are:
529. Lillian Margaret Berkey,[6] b. Nov. 23, 1858 (721).
530. John William Berkey,[6] b. Feb. 26, 1866.
531. Rosalie May Berkey,[6] b. Dec. 8, 1867 (723).
532. Lula Belle Berkey,[6] b. Jan. 21, 1870.

241. Ann E. Baker[5] m. ——— Rosenberger, a farmer, in Ohio, on Oct. 29, 1859.

Their children are:
533. William Clayton Rosenberger,[6] b. Jan. 18, 1864 (724).
534. Mary Alice Rosenberger,[6] b. Sept. 12, 1865 (724).
535. Henry Harley Rosenberger,[6] b. June 12, 1872.
536. John Elmer Rosenberger,[6] b. July 2, 1880.

THE GENEALOGY OF THE STEINER FAMILY. 71

242. John W. Baker,[5] farmer in Ohio, m. Elmira Michaels on Sept. 29, 1863.

Their children are:
537. Anna L. Baker,[6] b. Feb. 25, 1865. d. Nov. 21, 1881.
538. Olive E. Baker,[6] b. Nov. 3, 1868. d. Apr. 23, 1888.
539. H. M. Baker,[6] b. Dec. 3, 1877. d. Dec. 21, 1879.
540. Ethel C. Baker,[6] b. Dec. 24, 1882.
541. Edith W. Baker,[6] b. Dec. 24, 1882.

243. Wm. H. Baker,[5] farmer in Ohio, m. Carter Elizabeth Keller on Dec. 26, 1871.

Their children are:
542. Homer K. Baker,[6] b. Nov. 10, 1873.
543. Lulu D. Baker,[6] b. Oct. 25, 1875.
544. Lewis W. Baker,[6] b. Jan. 7, 1886.

244. Mary J. Baker[5] m. Leroy J. Michaels, farmer, of Seneca Co., Ohio, on Oct. 8, 1866.

Their children are:
545. Ola Belle Michaels,[6] b. Aug. 18, 1868.
546. Courtland Leroy Michaels,[6] b. Apr. 17, 1870. Connected with Sun Oil Co.
547. William Hallie Michaels,[6] b. Aug. 16, 1872. (B. A. Wooster University) Lawyer.
548. Margaret Eliza Michaels,[6] b. Oct. 7, 1875.
549. John Michaels,[6] b. Nov. 23, 1881.
550. Bessie Michaels,[6] b. Aug. 23, 1884. d. Aug. 22, 1885.
551. Corinne Michaels,[6] b. May 9, 1889.

246. Alice S. Baker[5] m. John Wm. Keller, farmer, in Ohio, Oct. 8, 1872.

Their children are:
552. Rolla Baker Keller,[6] b. Jan. 19, 1875. d. Aug. 22, 1875.
553. Leonard B. Keller,[6] b. Dec. 1, 1876.
554. Bertha Jane Keller,[6] b. July 1, 1879.
555. Grace Hibshman Keller,[6] b. Aug. 31, 1883.
556. William Arthur Keller,[6] b. Mch. 13, 1887.

248. Charles Winecaff[5] m. ———. Lives in California.
556-1.

250. Emma Winecaff⁶ m. J. Johnson, of Berlin, Penn.
557.

251. Anna Winecaff⁶ m. ———.
558.

254. Ann S. Fackender⁶ m. J. W. Haskins (b. June 29, 1858) on Nov. 27, 1884, at Reid City, Mich. They live at Du Boise, Clearfield Co., Pa. He is a barber. They have no children.

255. Victoria A. Fackender⁶ m. John E. Harnish (b. Mch. 7, 1854) on Mch. 30, 1876. He is a farmer in Sligo, Clarion Co., Pa.

Their children are:
559. Burr Harnish,⁷ b. Dec. 28, 1879.
560. John Andrew Harnish,⁷ b. Dec. 23, 1883.
561. Horatio S. Harnish,⁷ b. June 18, 1885.
562. Eugene I. Harnish,⁷ b. Nov. 16, 1887.

257. George W. Fackender,⁶ residing at Sligo, without occupation, m. July 4, 1878, Sadie J. Galbreath (b. Feb. 6, 1853).

Their children are:
563. Robert J. Fackender,⁷ b. Apr. 15, 1879.
564. Maggie M. Fackender,⁷ b. May 10, 1881.
565. Susannah E. Fackender,⁷ b. Mch. 25, 1884.
566. William F. Fackender,⁷ b. June 5, 1887.
567. Leah E. Fackender,⁷ b. Jan. 3, 1891.

258. Chas. F. Stoner,⁶ carpenter and builder, of Oil City, Venango Co., Penn., m. Sept. 19, 1886, Mary M. Sherman.

Their children are:
568. Margaret Beulah Stoner,⁷ b. Mch. 6, 1888.
569. Sarah Mabel Stoner,⁷ b. Dec. 30, 1890.
570. Amy Sherman Stoner,⁷ b. Sept. 6, 1892.

265. Lucy M. Thompson⁶ m. Curtis Somerville, carpenter, of Coreapolis, Allegheny Co., Penn., on Dec. 13, 1883.

Their children are:
571. Alice Huldah Somerville,⁷ b. Jan. 24, 1884.
572. Edith Lilian Somerville,⁷ b. July 25, 1885.

268. Anna L. Stoner⁶ m. Edward F. Kerr (b. Aug. 11, 1858), farmer,

THE GENEALOGY OF THE STEINER FAMILY.   73

of Rimersburg, Clarion Co., Penn., on Jan. 1, 1880. They now live in Kansas.

Their children are:
573. Blanche Kerr,[7] b. Mch. 12, 1881, in Clarion Co. d. Sept. 9, 1881.
574. Louie N. Kerr,[7] b. July 16, 1882, in Pottawattamie Co., Kan.
575. Thomas S. Kerr,[7] b. Mch. 14, 1885, in Riley Co., Kansas.
576. Oakley H. Kerr,[7] b. May 22, 1891, in Jefferson Co., Kan.

269. Hannah Margaret Stoner[6] m. —— Hoover.
577.

272. R. G. Stoner,[6] of Erie, Pa., m. Etta Rankin on Aug. 11, 1892.
578.

274. David Stoner[6] m. Agnes Harrison (b. June 17, 1861, in Clarion Co.) on Oct. 18, 1881. He is a farmer, residing in Knoxdale, Jefferson Co., Penn.

Their children are:
579. Francis Merl Stoner,[7] b. July 21, 1883.
580. Bessie Vera Stoner,[7] b. Dec. 26, 1886.
581. Edward Gay Stoner,[7] b. Oct. 31, 1889.
582. Margaret Blanche Stoner,[7] b. Mch. 20, 1891.

275. Flora L. Stoner[6] m. Sylvester Travis, of Wesleyville, Erie Co., Pa., on Aug. 31, 1882.

Their children are:
583. Francis Hurlbert Travis,[7] b. July 24, 1883.
584. Guy Winsworth Travis,[7] b. Dec. 17, 1887.
585. Edie Roy Travis,[7] b. Aug. 11, 1890. d. Aug. 20, 1891.

280. Henry C. Shaw,[6] civil engineer, residing at Homestead, Pa., m. Oct. 1, 1889, Fanny Patchen, of New York City.

Their children are:
586. Katharine Lydia Shaw,[7] b. Oct. 25, 1890.
587. Martha Shaw,[7] b. Feb. 11, 1892.

282. Margaret W. Shaw[6] m. Nov. 15, 1889, Geo. R. Lawrence, of Pittsburg, Pa., att'y-at-law (b. ——; d. Nov. 10, 1891). They had no children.

290. Frank R. Stoner, attorney-at-law, of Pittsburg, Pa., m. July 31, 1894, Sadie McCleery.

297. Katharine Stoner⁶ m. ———.
588.

302. Fannie Conrad⁶ m. ——— Allchesky, of Frederick City, on ———.
Their children are:
589. Emma A. Allchesky,⁷ b. ———.
590. Robert James Allchesky,⁷ b. ———.
591. William Franklin Allchesky,⁷ b. ———.

304. Ann C. Conrad⁶ m. Elmer Hardman.
592.

305. Melissa V. Steiner⁶ m. Wm. Riley, of Brooklyn, N. Y.
593.

306. Sophia Steiner⁶ m. Robert Davies (b. ———, d. ———).
594.

307. Anna M. Steiner⁶ m. John Billy.
Their children are:
595. Harry Billy,⁷ b. ———.
596. Clarence Billy,⁷ b. ———.

308. Alice Steiner⁶ m. Marshall Bartholow.
597.

319. Valetta Steiner⁶ m. Chas. E. H. Holmes, of Washington, D. C., on Nov. 4, 1867 (b. ———; d. ———, 18—).
Their children are:
598. Alice E. J. Holmes,⁷ b. ——— (726).
599. Grace Isabella Holmes,⁷ b. ———.
600. Charles Edwin Holmes,⁷ b. ———.
601. William John Holmes,⁷ b. ———.
602. Lucy Eleanora Holmes,⁷ b. ———.

320. Alice Steiner⁶ m. Capt. Francis Shamberg, of Buckhannan, W. Va., on Aug. 21, 1861. He was captain 1st Md. Cavalry U. S. Volunteers.
Their child is:
603. David Francis Shamberg,⁷ b. Aug. 13, 1862 (727).

THE GENEALOGY OF THE STEINER FAMILY. 75

322. Grace F. Steiner[6] m. Charles Pouder, clerk in the B. & O. office, Baltimore.

Their child is:
604. David Steiner Pouder,[7] b. Oct. 31, 1886.

325. Susan A. Steiner[6] m. Calvin A. Rhodes, of Frederick City, on Oct. 15, 1872.

Their children are:
605. Anne Grace Rhodes,[7] b. ———, 1873.
606. John Albert Rhodes,[7] b. ———, 1878.

326. Charles H. Steiner,[6] machinist, of Dayton, O., m. Laura W. Mumma, Sept. 26, 1872. They have no children.

329. Ira F. Steiner,[6] clerk in B. & O. freight office, Baltimore, Md., m. Irene Ruse on Nov. 2, 1886.

Their child is:
607. Donald Edward Steiner,[7] b. Aug. 10, 1888.

331. Fannie E. Steiner[6] m. Oscar Firetone, machinist, of Hanover, Pa., and Baltimore, Md., on Nov. 19, 1885. They have no children.

338. Millard F. Steiner[6] m. on Mch. 26, 1879, Lida Griffith. He is a ———, residing at Fostoria, Ohio.

Their children are:
608. Arthur Steiner,[7] b. Mch. 14, 1880. d. Oct. 3, 1880.
609. Pearl Steiner,[7] b. Aug. 24, 1881.
610. Harry I. Steiner,[7] b. Mch. 8, 1885.
611. Clarence P. Steiner,[7] b. Aug. 23, 1894.

340. Carrie Steiner[6] m. Samuel M. Lambright on Mch. 4, 1885.

Their children are:
612. Hazel Lambright,[7] b. Aug. 6, 1887 (dau.).
613. Harvey Lambright,[7] b. Sept. 5, 1889.

344. Wm. C. Steiner,[6] dealer in real estate in New York City, m. Ida Colton on Nov. 19, 1873.

Their children are:
614. Marion Colton Steiner,[7] b. Oct. 10, 1874 (dau.).
615. Margaret Hart Steiner,[7] b. Dec. 16, 1881.

THE GENEALOGY OF THE STEINER FAMILY.

349. Lilian C. Steiner⁶ m. Dec. 4, 1884, Thos. Rice, of Frederick City.

Their children are:
616. Anna Othetta Rice,⁷ b. Oct. 30, 1887.
617. Mary Louise Rice,⁷ b. June 28, 1891. d. Nov. 1, 1891.
618. Jane Elizabeth Rice,⁷ b. June 28, 1891.

351. Francis M. Steiner,⁶ of Point Pleasant, Ocean Co., N. J., m. Florence Estelle Ott, Oct. 31, 1883.

Their children are:
619. Lewis Marshall Steiner,⁷ b. Sept. 15, 1884, at Pt. Pleasant. d. Aug. 23, 1885.
620. Emma May Steiner,⁷ b. Apr. 23, 1885, at Pt. Pleasant.
621. William Henry Steiner,⁷ b. Jan. 29, 1888, at Pt. Pleasant.

353. Orlean M. Steiner⁶ m. Wm. H. Darner, of Frederick City, in Washington, D. C., on Sept. 8, 1889.

Their child is:
622. Hazel May Darner,⁷ b. Aug. 21, 1890, in Frederick.

354. Gracy Steiner⁶ m. Wm. H. Melchoir, of Washington, D. C., on Sept. 26, 1889.

Their child is:
623. Marian Catharine Melchoir,⁷ b. Apr. 19, 1890, in Washington.

358. David Steiner⁶ m. Dec. 20, 1895, Sophia Shoemaker. He lives in Frederick and is a brick-maker.

363. Ida. V. Cramer⁶ m. Feb. 15, 1882, Mathias E. Bartgis, of Frederick City. They had no children.

364. Cora M. Cramer⁶ m. Franklin Pierce Miller, of Frederick City, on Jan. 20, 1876.

Their children are:
624. Lillie May Miller,⁷ b. Mch. 2, 1877.
625. Franklin Davis Miller,⁷ b. ———.
626. William Allen Miller,⁷ b. ———.
627. Matthias Bartgis Miller,⁷ b. ———.
628. Harry Walter Miller,⁷ b. ———.

THE GENEALOGY OF THE STEINER FAMILY. 77

629. Susan Rebecca Miller,⁷ b. ———.
630. Ida Belle Miller,⁷ b. ———.

365. Joseph C. Cramer⁶ m. Loretta Derffey on Sept. 13, 1881.
Their children are:
631. Bessie May Cramer,⁷ b. ———.
632. Joseph Franklin Cramer,⁷ b. ———.
633. Annie May Cramer,⁷ b. ———.
634. Charlotte Sophia Cramer,⁷ b. ———.
635. Ida Virginia Cramer,⁷ b. ———.

368. Eli H. Cramer⁶ m. Sarah Bruchey, Apr. 7, 1891. He lives in Frederick City.

369. Edward A. Cramer⁶ m. Harriet V. Koogle.
Their children are:
636. Ethan Allen Cramer,⁷ b. ———.
637. Ralph William Cramer,⁷ b. ———.

370. Charles F. Cramer⁶ m. Lulu E. Lambert on Sept. 30, 1891.
Their child is:
638. Charles Edward Cramer,⁷ b. ———.

378. Steiner Schley,⁶ apothecary, of Frederick City, Md., m. Lilian Kunkel on Jan. 28, 1885. He is a director of the Fredericktown Savings Institution.
Their children are:
639. Rebecca Steiner Schley,⁷ b. Nov. 2, 1886. d. Sept. 29, 1892.
640. Lilian Kunkel Schley,⁷ b. Jan. 24, 1888.
641. Lewis Fairfax Schley,⁷ b. July 9, 1889. d. Dec. 22, 1891.
642. John Reading Schley,⁷ b. Oct. 12, 1894.

379. Jennie Schley⁶ m. Wm. H. Miller (b. Mch., 1838) on Sept. 29, 1875. He lives in Frederick City and is teller in the Frederick County National Bank. They have no children.

388. Edward Derr Shriner,⁶ of Ceresville, Frederick Co., miller, m. Nannie May Getzendanner⁶ (427) on Dec. 17, 1890 (b. May 28, 1867).

393. Frances Leiter⁶ m. T. W. Hays, of Tolono, Ill.
643.

394. Edward T. Leiter,[6] dentist, m. Florence Riser, of Dayton, Ind.
644.

396. Lewis H. Leiter[6] m. Sylvia Annan, of Tolono, Ill.
645.

397. John W. Leiter[6] m. Matilda Swarts, of Decatur, Ill.
646.

400. Charles E. Leiter,[6] railroad engineer, m. Nellie Toffehmeyer, of Mason City, Iowa.
647.

402. John W. Getzendanner[6] m. [1] Isidore Fout on ———, 1867 (b. ———, 18—; d. ———, 18—); [2] Martha V. Getzendanner[5] (176) on ———, 18— (b. Jan. 29, 1839; d. ———, 1878); [3] Melissa Hewitt on ———. He is a physician, residing at Middletown, Md.

Child of J. W. and Isidore (Fout) Getzendanner:
648. Harvey Fout Getzendanner,[7] b. Oct. 17, 1868, dentist and homœopathic physician.

Child of J. W. and M. V. (Getzendanner) Getzendanner:
649. Harriet Getzendanner,[7] b. July 23, 1874.

403. Samuel P. Getzendanner[6] m. Anna May Zimmerman on Nov. 21, 1872. He was a farmer, residing on the old homestead in Frederick Co.

Their children are:
650. Edith Regina Getzendanner,[7] b. Nov. 21, 1877.
651. Harriet Elizabeth Getzendanner,[7] b. Aug. 31, 1879.

408. Mollie Bechtol[6] m. James Williams. He is a farmer and stockraiser in Bosque Co., Texas.
652.

409. Fannie Bechtol[6] m. Andrew Holmerk. He is a farmer in Bosque Co., Texas.
653.

410. Elizabeth F. Hughes[6] m. D. C. Wilcoxon[6] (435) on Apr. —, 1875. He is a merchant of Baltimore, Md.

THE GENEALOGY OF THE STEINER FAMILY. 79

Their children are:
654. Myrtle Wilcoxon,[7] b. Jan. 10, 1876.
655. Minette Wilcoxon,[7] b. Aug. 9, 1877.
656. Irvin Jackson Wilcoxon,[7] b. Nov. 12, 1881.

411. Wendell Hughes,[6] commission merchant, Baltimore, m. Hallie Cramer on May —, 1876.

Their children are:
657. Alice Catharine Hughes,[7] b. July 5, 1881.
658. Charles Reginald Hughes,[7] b. Dec., 1882.
659. George Leyburn Hughes,[7] b. Feb. 26, 1887.

412. Wm. S. Hughes, commission merchant, Baltimore, m. Elizabeth F. Manning on ———, 1877.

Their children are:
660. Mabel Hughes,[7] b. ———.
661. Ethel Rebecca Hughes,[7] b. ———.
662. Raymond Hughes,[7] b. ———.
663. Lillian Hughes,[7] b. ———.
664. William Hughes,[7] b. ———.

413. Florence P. Hughes[6] m. Samuel Gill (b. June 10, 1868), of Baltimore, on ———, 1892.
665.

414. Virginia Getzendanner[6] m. T. W. Obenderfer on ———.

Their children are:
666. Nellie Obenderfer,[7] b. ———.
667. William Obenderfer,[7] b. ———.

416. Florence Getzendanner[6] m.
668.

417. Estelle Getzendanner[6] m. ———.
669.

418. Minnie Getzendanner[6] m. ——— Sheffler, of Frederick City.
670.

422. Laura V. Getzendanner[6] m. Nelson Diehl (b. June 13, 1839) on

———, 1870. He is a farmer in Frederick County. They have no children.

423. Winton E. Getzendanner,[5] of Chicago, Ill., m. Lulu A. Clancy on ———, 1883. They have no children.

424. Daniel J. Getzendanner,[6] of Montgomery Co., Md., m. Jennie Schaefer on Nov. 18, 1891 (b. Oct. 17, 1863).
671.

425. Wm. R. Getzendanner,[6] farmer, of Montgomery Co., Md., m. ———, 1881, Belle Ramsburg.

Their child is:
672. Maude May Getzendanner,[7] b. Sept. 29, 1886.

426. Addie E. Getzendanner[6] m. Roderick A. Barrick, dentist, of Newark, Ohio.

Their children are:
673. Lulu Mary Barrick,[7] b. July 26, 1885.
674. Helen Ashton Barrick,[7] b. Oct. 20, 1887. d. Apr. 23, 1890.

428. Charles C. Getzendanner,[6] farmer, of Jefferson Co., W. Va., m. ———, 1881, Lilly Thomas (b. ———; d. Aug. —, 1884).

429. Clara C. Getzendanner[6] m. D. W. Border, A. B., A. M., M. D., of Jefferson Co., W. Va., on Mch. 24, 1880.

Their children are:
675. Daniel Worth Border,[7] b. Jan. 4, 1881. d. May 1, 1881.
676. Ralph Winebrenner Border,[7] b. Feb. 3, 1882.
677. Mark Getzendanner Border,[7] b. Oct. 23, 1886. d. July 30, 1887.
678. William Meade Border,[7] b. Dec. 29, 1888. d. Feb. 18, 1890.

430. Henry C. Getzendanner,[6] attorney-at-law, of ———, W. Va., m. on Nov. 28, 1882, Anna Jacqueline Morgan, daughter Col. Wm. A. Morgan, of W. Va. (b. Nov. 3, 1861).

Their child is:
679. William Jacqueline Getzendanner,[7] b. Nov. 3, 1890.

436. Wm. Wilcoxon[6] m. Elizabeth C. Keller (b. Sept. 17, 1858) on May 22, 1883. He has been a lawyer and ironfounder, residing at Frederick City.

THE GENEALOGY OF THE STEINER FAMILY. 81

Their children are:
681. Mary Marcia Wilcoxon,⁷ b. May 18, 1884.
682. William Wilcoxon,⁷ b. Aug. 24, 1885. d. Apr. 23, 1886.
683. Wilbur Wilcoxon,⁷ b. Jan. 2, 1887.
684. Ruth Elizabeth Wilcoxon,⁷ b. Jan. 17, 1888.
685. DeWitt Keller Wilcoxon,⁷ b. June 22, 1891.

438. Clara Wilcoxon⁶ m. Elmer Brown, Mch. 11, 1885.

Their children are:
686. Jane Brown,⁷ b. May 10, 1886.
687. Anna Brown,⁷ b. Nov. 22, 1887.
688. Samuel Brown,⁷ b. Jan. 15, 1889.

442. Lelia Getzendanner⁶ m. ———, lawyer, of Fort Worth, Texas.
689.

444. Minnie Getzendanner⁶ m. ——— Johnson.

Their child is:
690. Daughter.

453. Katie E. Getzendanner⁶ m. Edward Dawson Grove, of Frederick City, on Oct. 31, 1894.
691.

460. Lily M. Scholl⁶ m. Frank J. Schroeder, of Frederick City, on ———, 1885.

Their children are:
692. Harry Oscar Schroeder,⁷ b. ———, 1887.
693. Frank J. Schroeder,⁷ b. ———, 1889.
694. Miriam Schroeder,⁷ b. ———, 1891.

479-1. Geo. W. Bright,⁶ vice-president Sunday Creek Coal Company, and merchant, Columbus, Ohio, m. Martha Morrel.

Their child is:
694-1. Mary Louisa Bright,⁷ b. ———, 1878.

479-2. Mary E. Bright⁶ m. July 11, 1872, Thomas Pittman, a farmer, of Hammond, Kansas (b. Dec. 2, 1842).

Their children were:

694-2. Mary Cleone Pittman,⁷ b. May 23, 1873.
694-3. George Bright Pittman,⁷ b. Jan. 5, 1876. d. Aug. 1, 1882.
694-4. Agnes Theo Pittman,⁷ b. Feb. 28, 1879. d. July 25, 1882.
694-5. Samuel Wishard Pittman,⁷ b. July 1, 1881. d. July 31, 1882.
694-6. Thomas Lawrence Pittman,⁷ b. Mch. 4, 1883.
694-7. Martha Sophia Pittman,⁷ b. Nov. 9, 1885.

479-6. William G. Souder⁶ m. Katharine ———.

Their child was:
694-8. John Winfield Scott Souder,⁷ b. Oct. 25, 1888. d. June 26, 1892.

479-8. Samuel E. S. Bright⁶ m. ———.

Their children are:
694-9. John Z. Bright,⁷ b. ———, 1879.
694-10. Walter S. Bright,⁷ b. ———, 1881.

479-9. Anna A. Bright⁶ m. W. N. Miller, a lawyer, of Parkersburg, W. Va.

Their child is:
694-11. Louisa B. Miller,⁷ b. ———, 1881.

479-10. Rev. Jesse Levi Bright⁶ m. July, 1891, Florence Beard. He is pastor at Columbus, Ohio. (Yale Divinity School, 1890.)

Their children are:
694-12. Ruth H. Bright,⁷ b. ———.
694-13. Esther Bright,⁷ b. ———.

479-11. Col. Elsworth Bright,⁶ wholesale millinery merchant, Columbus, Ohio, m. Elida May King.

Their child is:
694-14. Helen Bright,⁷ b. ———, 1889.

479-14. Cora V. Stoner⁶ m. Dec., 1879, David Hamilton (b. Dec. 6, 1851).

Their children are:
694-15. Howard Douglas Hamilton,⁷ b. Dec. 22, 1880. d. Oct. 2, 1881.
694-16. Evelyn Stuart Hamilton,⁷ b. Mch. 10, 1884.
694-17. Arthur Milton Hamilton,⁷ b. Nov. 1, 1888.
694-18. David G. Hamilton,⁷ b. Aug. 17, 1891.
694-19. Cora Campbell Hamilton,⁷ b. July 19, 1895. d. July 20, 1895.

THE GENEALOGY OF THE STEINER FAMILY.   83

479-17. Lillie D. Newcomb⁶ m. ———, 1881, Edwin Vance, a druggist, of Westerville, Ohio. She is a milliner. They have no children.

479-18. Nellie E. Newcomb⁶ m. ———, 1884, Harry Clippinger, who is in a building and loan association at Delaware, Ohio.

Their children are:
694-20. Lillian Clippinger,⁷ b. ———, 1886.
694-21. Martha Clippinger,⁷ b. ———, 1891.

479-20. Fred. Newcomb⁶ m. ———, 1892, Mary Whitney He is a railroadman at Columbus, Ohio.

Their child is:
694-22. Charlotte A. Newcomb,⁷ b. Feb. 28, 1894.

479-24. Mary Elizabeth Stoner,⁶ of Gothenburg, Nebraska, m. L. C. McBride, July 4, 1869.

Their children are:
694-22-1. Jason E. McBride,⁷ b. Sept. 18, 1870 (730).
694-22-2. Orien W. McBride,⁷ b. Apr. 15, 1875 (731).
694-22-3. Effie McBride,⁷ b. Jan. 19, 1882.
694-22-4. Maude McBride,⁷ b. Mch. 31, 1889.

479-24-1. Aaron E. Stoner,⁶ of Gothenburg, Nebraska, m. Maggie E. Griffith, July 4, 1872.

479-24-5. Alverda L. Stoner,⁶ of Gothenburg, Nebraska. m. J. A. Emmert, Aug. 12, 1878.

Their children are:
694-22-5. Chester S. Emmert,⁷ b. Sept. 17, 1879.
694-22-6. Walter E. Emmert,⁷ b. Dec. 28, 1881.
694-22-7. Roy Raymond Emmert,⁷ b. Nov. 25, 1886. d. ———, 1888.
694-22-8. Clarence J. E. Emmert,⁷ b. Mch. 17, 1889.

479-24-6. Adah Z. Stoner,⁶ of Gothenburg, Nebraska, m. A. B. Hann, Dec. 24, 1883.

Their children are:
694-22-9.   Aaron Ernest Hann,⁷ b. Nov. 6, 1886.
694-22-10. Arthur Harold Hann,⁷ b. Oct. 23, 1887. d. July 27, 1889.

479-24-7. Emma R. Stoner,⁶ of Gothenburg, Nebraska, m. J. W. Snyder.

Their children are:
694-22-11. Roscoe Everett Snyder,⁷ b. June 6, 1891.
694-22-12. Roy Lester Snyder,⁷ b. Dec. 19, 1892.
694-22-13. Raymond Wesley Snyder,⁷ b. Dec. 19, 1892. d. ———, 1893.
694-22-14. Lewis Wilbur Snyder,⁷ b. Aug. 2, 1894.

479-25. Mary Cromwell⁶ m. Oct. 10, 1866, Philip King (b. Dec. 25, 1841), of Marengo, Iowa.

Their children are:
694-23-1. Clara King,⁷ b. Sept. 12, 1867 (731).
694-23-2. Margaret King,⁷ b. Nov. 10, 1868.
694-23-3. Emanuel King,⁷ b. Dec. 23, 1870 (732).
694-23-4. Marcenia King,⁷ b. Feb. 20, 1872 (733).
694-23-5. Annie King,⁷ b. Nov. 28, 1873. d. Dec. 2, 1873.
694-23-6. William King,⁷ b. Nov. 16, 1874.
694-23-7. Lauretto King,⁷ b. July 31, 1876.
694-23-8. Annie King,⁷ b. Apr. 5, 1877.
694-23-9. Leo King,⁷ b. Dec. 16, 1880.
694-23-10. Joseph King,⁷ b. Jan. 17, 1881.
694-23-11. Susan King,⁷ b. June 12, 1882.
694-23-12. Celia King,⁷ b. Jan. 10, 1884.
694-23-13. John King,⁷ b. Oct. 13, 1886.

479-26. Catharine E. Stoner⁶ m. William Clyde, farmer, living in Ladora, Iowa.

479-26-1. Dennis L. Stoner⁶ m. Cina Huddleston. He is a farmer in Ladora, Iowa.

479-26-2. Clara M. Stoner⁶ m. Christian Keil, farmer, living in Ladora, Iowa.

479-26-3. Almeda A. Stoner⁶ m. John Keil, farmer, living in Ladora, Iowa.

479-26-4. Theodore D. Stoner⁶ m. Minnie Beemer. He is a farmer, living in Ladora, Iowa.

479-26-5. George N. Stoner⁶ m. Ada Rosenberger. He is a farmer, living in Ladora, Iowa.

THE GENEALOGY OF THE STEINER FAMILY.   85

479-27-2. Anna M. Stoner⁶ m. Apr. 10, 1875, Charles O. Niles (b. May 1, 1852), of Tiffin, Ohio.

Their child is:
694-24. Rushton D. Niles,⁷ b. Aug. 30, 1879.

479-36. Jessie Oram⁶ m. Dr. ——— Collins, of Dayton, Ohio.

Their children are:
694-25. Helen Collins,⁷ b. ———.
694-26. Herbert Collins,⁷ b. ———.

479-37. Glenna Oram⁶ m. Moses Schwab, of Dayton, Ohio.
694-27.

480. Jesse L. Stoner⁶ m. Nov. —, 1889, Florence Boner. He is a jeweler and printer, residing at Larned, Kansas.

Their children are:
695. Frank N. Stoner,⁷ b. Nov. —, 1890.
695-1. Ruth Stoner,⁷ b. July —, 1894.

481. Elizabeth Eader⁶ m. Philip Vanfossen, of Newark, Ohio.
696. They have one daughter.

483. Lewis Wm. Eader⁶ m. Sally ———. He is a farmer in Brownsville, Tenn.

Their children are:
697. Josella Eader⁷ (daughter), b. ———.
698. Pauline Eader,⁷ b. ———.
699. Lewis Eader,⁷ b. ———.
700. Howell Eader,⁷ b. ———.
701. (son) Eader,⁷ b. ———.
702. (son) Eader,⁷ b. ———.

486. Chas. Elmer Eader,⁶ of Frederick City, m. Mary Quinn.

Their children are:
703. Emma May Eader,⁷ b. ———.
704. Charles Eader,⁷ b. ———.

505. Laura V. Repp⁶ m. Jan. 14, 1894, Frederick Frick, marshal of Tiffin, Ohio. They have no children.

508. Ada Maule⁶ m. John Snyder in ——, 1883.

Their children are:
705. William Raymond Snyder,⁷ b. July, 1886.
706. Grace May Snyder,⁷ b. May, 1889.
707. Mabel Snyder,⁷ b. Dec. 12, 1891.

514. Victoria Maule⁶ m. Aaron Zink.

Their children are:
708.
709.

515. Laura J. Maule⁶ m. ——, Henry Zink.

Their child is:
710. Lola Zink, b. ——, 1881.

515. Didanna A. Maule⁶ m. George McNut. They have no children.

516. John B. Maule,⁶ school-teacher, of Ohio, m. Vienna Mull. They have no children.

517. Ellen R. Derr⁶ m. Edward T. Swander, Nov. 20, 1877.

Their children are:
711. Nettie M. Swander,⁷ b. Dec. 5, 1878.
712. Vernie E. Swander,⁷ b. June 6, 1881.
713. Ira A. Swander,⁷ b. Sept. 22, 1882.
714. Clara D. Swander,⁷ b. July 7, 1884.

518. Wm. A. Derr⁶ m. Mattie Knepple, Nov. 10, 1887. He is a farmer.

Their child is:
715. Perry Derr,⁷ b. Dec. 30, 1892.

519. Hiram G. Park⁶ m. Eleanor M. Franz, Dec. 27, 1881. He is a hardware merchant.

They have one son:
716. Harry Richmond Park,⁷ b. Nov. 25, 1882.

522. John C. Park⁶ m. Flora R. Wendler, Oct. 12, 1887. He is a hardware merchant.

They have one son:

THE GENEALOGY OF THE STEINER FAMILY. 87

717. Arthur Wendler Park, b. May 10, 1892.

522. Anna Park⁶ m. Thomas E. Crank, Jan. 2, 1884.
Their children are:
718. Elbert James Crank,⁷ b. Oct. 12, 1884.
719. Lula Catharine Crank,⁷ b. Mch. 24, 1891.

523. Charles E. Derr⁶ m. Annie Martin, Sept. 13, 1893. He is a lawyer.
They have a son:
720. ———— Derr,⁷ b. Oct. 14, 1894.

529. Lilian M. Berkey⁷ m. Sept. 14, 1886, Clarence Rickenbaugh, lawyer.
Their children are:
721. Robert Berkey Rickenbaugh,⁷ b. Oct. 3, 1887.
722. Margaret Rickenbaugh,⁷ b. Feb. 15, 1889.

531. Rosalie Berkey⁶ m. June 29, 1893, Frank Rickenbaugh, lawyer.
723.

533. William C. Rosenberger⁶ m. Feb. 28, 1890, Alice W. Bargen. They have no children.

534. Mary A. Rosenberger⁶ m. Ralph J. Van Buskirk, Nov. 9, 1886.
Their children are:
724. Dorsey Rosenberger Van Buskirk,⁷ b. Nov. 28, 1889.
725. Helen Baker Van Buskirk,⁷ b. Feb. 28, 1893.

598. Alice E. J. Holmes⁷ m. Linwood Lee Holbrook.
Their child is:
726. Almira Valletta Holbrook,⁸ b. ————.

603. David F. Shamburg,⁷ of West Virginia, m. Margaret Fallon.
Their children are:
727. Alice Elizabeth Shamburg,⁸ b. ————.
728. Henry Francis Shamburg,⁸ b. ————.
729. Mary Tacey Shamburg,⁸ b. ————.

694-22-1. Jason E. McBride⁷ m. Flora Keihn, Nov., 1891.
730.

694-22-2. O. W. McBride⁷ m. Emma Walker, Nov. 1895.

694-23-1. Clara King⁷ m. Sept. 12, 1885, Henry Bangheart, son of George and Elizabeth.
731.

694-23-3. Emanuel King⁷ m. Janie Bowers, daughter of Jabus and Mary, Sept. 4, 1893.
732.

694-23-4. Marcenia King⁷ m. Eli Goodrich.
733.

INDEX.

I.—Descendants of Jacob Steiner bearing the family name.

A

Aaron E., 479-24-1.
Ada M., 216-10.
Adah Zillah, 479-24-6.
Alfred Montrose, 119.
Alice, 308.
" 320.
" B., 210-6.
" J., 185.
Almeda A., 479-26-3.
Almedia Susan, 102.
Alverda Leonora, 479-24-5.
Ambrose E. B., 270
Amy Louise, 376.
" Sherman, 570.
Anna, 210-6.
" Barbara, 23.
" L, 268.
" M, 479-27-2.
" " 479-30.
" Margaret, 120.
" May, 307.
" Rebecca, 479-24-3.
Ann Eliza, 189-3.
" Elizabeth, 67.
" " 82.
" " 87.
" " 204-3.
" Marie, 204-4.
" Rebecca, 86.
" " 204.
" " 357.
" " Louisa, 140.
" Sophia, 204-1.
Annette Catharine, 335.
Arthur, 608.
Aurelia Eliza, 291.

B

Barbara Ann Elizabeth, 134.
Benedict, 4.
" 18.
Bernard Christian, 371.
Bertha Rebecca, 374.
" Virginia, 355.
Bessie Vera, 580.
Blanche A., 210-8.

C

Calvin, 210-4.
" Myers, 324.
Caroline, 110.
Carrie Elizabeth, 340.
Catharine, 33.
" E., 479-26.
" Margaret, 11.
" Wolfe, 116.
Charity, 44.
" 125.
Charles, 147.
" A., 207.
" Flavius, 258.
" Henry, 326.
" A. Seay, 189-7.
" Reighley, 317.
" S., 271.
Charlotte, 29.
" 52.
" 204-7.
" E., 216-1.
Christian, 10.
" 12.
" 25.
" 42.
" C., 84.

Christina, 28.
Clara Hauer, 343.
" M., 479-26-2.
Clarence P., 611.
Clark, 480-3.
Cora O., 210-11.
" V., 479-14.

D

Daisy Yarborough, 247.
Daniel, 53.
" Hicks, 348.
" Nicholas, 132.
David, 31.
" 267.
" 274.
" 358.
" Christian, 128.
" Eshebman, 27.
Della B., 273.
Dennis, 88.
" Caspar, 89.
" L., 479-24-1.
" Eli, 479-24-4.
Denton, Lloyd, 130.
" Wiest, 318.
Donald Edward, 607.
Douglas A., 216-8..
Dow S., 216-4.

E

Eda S., 467-17.
Edgar C., 210-9.
Edmund Curtis, 293.
Edward Gay, 581.
" Everett, 332.
Elizabeth, 14.
" 16.
" 20.
" 34.
" 40.
" 115.
" 123.
" 137.
Ellen A., 210-2.
Elmira Elizabeth, 141.
Elriporter, 259.
Emma, 148.
" Jane, 333.
" M., 479-27-1.

Emma May, 620.
" Rosetta, 479-24-7.
Emmet C., 479-27-3.
Ettie, 181-3.
Eva, 294.
" K., 210-10.
Ezra, 37.

F

Fannie Elizabeth, 331.
" K., 216-9.
Flavius Josephus, 114.
" " 276.
Flora Lily, 275.
Florence A., 189.
" B., 216-13.
" Esther, 407-14.
" Gertrude, 183.
Francis Edwin, 214.
" " 480-4.
" Marion, 351.
" Merl, 579.
Frank Myers, 479-39.
" N., 695.
" Rahm, 290.
Frederick, 13.
" 30.
" 45.
" 64.
" Byerly, 54.

G

George, 51.
" 360.
" B., 210-12.
" F., 181.
" G., 467-1.
" Lewis, 463.
" N., 479-26-5.
" W., 80.
" W., 204-6.
" Washington, 205.
Georgiana, 99.
Gertrude Marie, 480-6.
" Rachel, 372.
Glenna M., 479-29.
Grace G., 467-1.
" Fetterhafen, 322.
Gracy, 354.

INDEX.

H

Hannah, 36.
" Margaret, 269.
" Maria, 111.
Harry J., 610.
" Stair, 356.
Hebron Cramer, 342.
Heiner Augustus, 113.
Helen Rebecca, 480-7.
Henrietta Virginia, 459.
" V., 209-1.
Henry, 3.
" 7.
" 22.
" 38.
" 83.
" 215.
" Christopher, 133.
" Otho, 350.
" Rohr, 345.
Herman Francis, 135.

I

Ida M., 261.
Ira Frank, 329.

J

Jacob, 1.
" 5.
" 26.
" 41.
" 43.
" Frederick, 131.
" Henry, 321.
" " 339.
James, 181-2.
" 203.
" Madison, 129.
" " 213.
" Oliver, 100.
Jesse, 66.
" 187.
" H. R. 210-5.
" Lee, 480-1.
Jessie W., 216-6.
John, 2.
" 6.
" 17.

John, 43.
" 81.
" Alexander, 129.
" " 213.
" A., 262.
" Edgar, 328.
" Eli, 206.
" Frederick, 62.
" Hurlburt, 277.
" S., 208-1.
" W., 189-1.
" Wesley, 109.
" William, 352.
Jonathan, 65.
Joseph H., 210-13.
Joshua, 68.

K

Kate Brunner, 330.
" O. Reese, 189-5.
Katharine, 297.

L

Laura, 182.
" C., 467-2.
" Lavinia, 189-4.
" Victoria, 216.
Lee Rowland, 480-5.
Lewis Henry, 139.
" Marshall, 619.
Lilian Catharine, 349.
Louisa Hart, 346.
Lucy T., 467-19.
Luther Edward, 336.

M

Mabel A., 479-31.
Marcus Woodward, 296.
Margaret, 63.
" Beulah, 568.
" Blanche, 582.
" Elizabeth, 107.
" " 122.
" Hart, 615.
Maria, 61.
" Magdalena, 15.
Marietta F., 210.
Marion Colton, 614.

INDEX.

Martha Emily, 479-24-2.
Mary, 8.
" 19.
" 181-4.
" Amelia, 327.
" Ann Cecilia, 126.
" Ellen, 98.
" " 334.
" Elizabeth, 479-24.
" " 323.
" Magdalen, 21.
" Margaret, 69.
" " 289.
" Margaretta, 189-2.
" Rose, 359.
Matilda Margaret, 138.
Maud O., 216-12.
May K., 467-18.
Melissa Virginia, 305.
Mertie M., 480-2.
Millard Francis, 338.
Milton, 204-5.

N

Nellie H., 216-7.
Norman, 186.

O

Oakley D., 216-11.
Orlean May, 353.
Oscar, 184.
Otterbein, 210-3.

P

Pearl, 609.

R

R. G., 272.
Raleigh G., 480.
Ralph, 216-14.
" Dunning Smyth, 375.
Richard S., 209.
Rodney Benedict, 246.
Roland, 361.
Royal G., 479-15.

Ruth, 695-1.
" E., 467-3.
" Rowland, 480-8.

S

Sallie, 181-5.
Samuel H., 208.
Sarah Mabel, 569.
Solomon, 35.
Sophia, 366.
Stephen, 9.
Susan, 347.
" Laura, 337.
" Rebecca, 136.
" Sophia, 325.
Susannah, 24.
" 85.
" 108.
" 216-3.
" M., 205-1.

T

Theodore D., 479-26-4.
Thomas C., 216.
" Stall, 112.

V

Valetta, 319.
Victoria, 118.
Virginia, 341.

W

Walter Ralph, 373.
Willia R., 216-5.
William, 124.
" Chapin, 344.
" Christian, 60.
" F., 479-13.
" H., 204-2.
" Henry, 127.
" " 621.
" Parker, 260.
" Randolph, 101.
" Wirt, 295.
Winfield Scott, 213-1.

INDEX. 93

II.—Descendants of Jacob Steiner bearing other family names.

A

Allchesky,
  Emma A., 589.
  Robert James, 590.
  William Franklin, 591.
Ashenhurst,
  Alice, 466.
  Florence Gertrude, 465.
  Harry, 464.

B

Baker,
  Alice Sophia, 245.
  Anna L., 537.
  Anne Elizabeth, 241.
  Edith W., 541.
  Elinore, 239.
  Ethel C., 540.
  H. M., 539.
  Homer K., 542.
  John Wesley, 242.
  Lewis W., 544.
  Lulu D., 543.
  Mary Isabelle, 244.
  Olive E., 538.
  Susan Emily, 240.
  William Henry, 243.
Barrick,
  Helen Ashton, 674.
  Lulu Mary, 673.
Bechtol,
  David, 167.
  Fannie, 170.
  Gilla, 168.
  Lewis, 166.
  Mollie, 169.
  Scott, 165.
Berkey,
  John William, 530.
  Lillian Margaret, 529.
  Lulu Belle, 532.
  Rosalie May, 531.
Billy,
  Clarence, 596.
  Harry, 595.

Border,
  Daniel Worth, 675.
  Mark Getzendanner, 677.
  Ralph Winebrenner, 676.
  William Meade, 678.
Brennan,
  Oscar, 467-5.
Bright,
  Anna A., 479-9.
  Elsworth, 479-11.
  Esther, 694-13.
  George W., 479-1.
  Helen, 694-14.
  Jesse Cleone, 479-12.
  "   Levi, 479-10.
  John L., 479-7.
  "   Z., 694-9.
  Mary E., 479-2.
  "   Louisa, 694-1.
  Ruth H., 694-12.
  Samuel E. S., 479-8.
  Walter S., 694-10.
Brown,
  Anna, 687.
  Jane, 686.
  Samuel, 688.

C

Carter,
  George S., 479.
Clemm,
  Anna Mary, 309.
  Charles McClellan, 315.
  Della, 312.
  Emma Henrietta, 313.
  Eugene Augustus, 316.
  Jeanette, 311.
  Julia, 314.
  Laura Virginia, 310.
Clippinger,
  Lillian, 694-20.
  Martha, 694-21.
Collins,
  Helen, 694-25.
  Herbert, 694-26.

INDEX.

Conrad,
  Ann Cadelia, 304.
  Ezra, 300.
  Fannie, 302.
  Henrietta, 301.
  Joseph, 303.
Cramer,
  Annie May, 633.
  Bessie May, 631.
  Charles Edward, 638.
  Charlotte Sophia, 634.
  Christian Francis, 370.
  Cora May, 364.
  Denton William, 362.
  Edward Allen, 369.
  Eli Henry, 368.
  Ethan Allen, 636.
  Ida Virginia, 363.
  " " 635.
  Joseph Carty, 365.
  " Franklin, 632.
  Ralph William, 637.
  Susan Phoebe, 367.
  Willie McClellan, 366.
Crank,
  Elbert James, 718.
  Lula Catharine, 719.
Cromwell,
  Mary, 479-25.

D

Darner,
  Hazel May, 622.
Derr,
  Annie, 521.
  Alice Virginia, 156.
  Belinda Catharine, 233.
  Clarinda Ann, 238.
  Catharine, 55.
  " E., 149.
  Charles Ezra, 523.
  " Worman, 159.
  David Henry, 237.
  Dennis Frederick, 234.
  Elizabeth, 57.
  " 95.
  Ellen R., 517.
  Eugene Lugenbeel, 157.
  Ezra, 96.

Derr,
  Ezra C., 527.
  " Zacharias, 160.
  Frances Elizabeth, 389.
  Frederick, 59.
  John, 56.
  " Peter, 152.
  " Thomas, 232.
  " Sebastian, 391.
  Kate Norman, 392.
  Margaret, 97.
  " Ann, 150.
  Mary, 58.
  Mary Louisa, 151.
  " Margaret, 235.
  Minnie, 525.
  Perry, 715.
  Rosanna Blanche, 526.
  Thomas Melanchthon, 153.
  W. H., 154.
  William, 236.
  " Addison, 518.
  " Reese, 158.
  Willie May, 390.
Dewald,
  Chauncey, 480-9.
  Paul, 480-10.
Durbin,
  Edward, 212.

E

Eader,
  Addie May, 487.
  Anna Mary, 220.
  Bessie Olivia, 497.
  Charles, 704.
  " 489.
  " Elmer, 486.
  " Ezra, 221.
  Daniel Root, 224.
  David Nicholas, 218.
  Eli Caspar, 93.
  Elizabeth, 481.
  Eliza Catharine, 217.
  Emma May, 703.
  Ezra Clifton, 485.
  George Diehl, 499.
  Howell, 700.
  Ida, 482.

INDEX. 95

Eader,
  Jonathan, 219.
  Josella, 697.
  Joseph, 488.
  Lewis, 699.
    " Benedict, 92.
    " Edmund, 490.
    " William, 483.
  Mary, 491.
  Pauline, 698.
  Pearl Alberta, 496.
  Peter Mantz, 225.
  Rachel Louisa, 223.
  Rondo Chalmers, 484.
  Walter Grason, 496.
    " Gregory, 493.
  William Henry, 222.
    "   " 492.
Emmert,
  Chester S., 694-22-5.
  Clarence J., 694-22-8.
  Roy R., 694-22-7.
  Walter E., 694-22-7.

F

Fackender,
  Ann Stoner, 254.
  Ella, 256.
  George Washington, 257.
  Leah E., 567.
  Maggie M., 564.
  Robert J., 563.
  Susannah E., 565.
  Victoria A., 255.
  William F., 566.
Fout,
  Ann Rebecca, 211.
Frazee,
  Katie Marie, 479-42.
Fredericks,
  Frank Alfred, 467-9.
  Kate Naomi, 467-8.
  Mary M., 467-6.
  William Harrison, 467-7.

G

Getzendanner,
  Addie E., 426.
  Anna Mary, 172.

Getzendanner,
  Anna Mary, 421.
  Ann Rebecca, 165.
  Arthur, 443.
  Bernard, 441.
  Bessie May, 455.
  Calvin Rose, 178.
  Catharine, 446.
    " Elizabeth, 161.
  Charles Christian, 428.
  Clara Catharine, 429.
    " Gertrude, 457.
  Daniel, 171.
    " J., 424.
  Eddie, 450.
  Edith Regina, 650.
  Edward Tabler, 169.
  Elizabeth, 170.
    " 415.
    " P., 448.
  Emma Grace, 456.
  Estelle, 417.
  Eugene, 451.
  Florence, 416.
  Francis Marion, 174.
  Franklin, 433.
  George H., 445.
    " W., 175.
  Harriet, 649.
    " Elizabeth, 651.
  Harrison, 177.
  Harvey Fout, 648.
  Henry Clay, 430.
  Jacob Reese, 167.
  Jennie, 420.
  John Augustus, 173.
    " Derr, 162.
    " William, 402.
  Kate Eugenia, 453.
  Katie, 449.
  Laura Virginia, 422.
  Lelia, 442.
  Lewis, 166.
  Lillian, 447.
  Louis David, 431.
  Martha Victoria, 176.
  Mary, 434.
    " Ann, 164.
    " Frank, 452.
  Maude May, 672.

Getzendanner,
    Milton Eugene, 179.
    Minnie, 418.
    " 444.
    Nannie May, 427.
    Nellie Clara, 454.
    Phoebe E., 432.
    Samuel Pettengall, 403.
    Susan Nixdorff, 458.
    Thomas, 168.
    Virginia, 414.
    William Abraham, 163.
    " Jacqueline, 679.
    " R., 425.
    Winfield, 419.
    Winton E., 423.
Graham,
    Donna Rosa, 264.

H

Hamilton,
    Arthur Milton, 694-17.
    Cora Campbell, 694-19.
    David G., 694-18.
    Evelyn Stuart, 694-16.
    Howard Douglas, 694-15.
Hann,
    Aaron E., 694-22-9.
    Arthur H., 694-22-10.
Hanshew,
    Caroline Virginia, 471.
    Charles Frederick, 469.
    Henry E., 191.
    " Muhlenberg, 472.
    John Keller, 468.
    Mary Catharine, 470.
Harnish,
    Burr, 559.
    Eugene I., 562.
    Horatio S., 561.
    John A., 560.
Hauser,
    Almedia Steiner, 106.
    Anna Steiner, 104.
    Marion, 105.
Herstine,
    May, 278.
    Solomon Stoner, 279.
Holbrook,
    Almira Valetta, 726.

Holmes,
    Alice E. J., 598.
    Charles Edwin, 600.
    Grace Isabella, 599.
    Lucy Eleanora, 602.
    William John, 601.
Hoye,
    Adolphus C., 252.
    Marion S., 253.
Hughes,
    Alice Catharine, 657.
    Charles Reginald, 658.
    Elizabeth F., 410.
    Ethel Rebecca, 661.
    Florence Patterson, 413.
    George Leyburn, 659.
    Lillian, 663.
    Mabel, 660.
    Raymond, 662.
    Wendell, 411.
    William, 664.
    " Samuel, 412.

K

Kegg,
    Horace Vergil, 467-10.
Keller,
    Bertha Jane, 554.
    Grace Hibshman, 555.
    Leonard B., 553.
    Rolla Baker, 552.
    William Arthur, 556.
Kerr,
    Blanche, 573.
    Louie N., 574.
    Oakley H., 576.
    Thomas S., 575.
King,
    Annie, 694-23-5.
    " 694-23-8.
    Celia, 694-23-12.
    Clara, 694-23-1.
    Emmanuel, 694-23-3.
    John, 694-23-13.
    Joseph, 694-23-10.
    Lauretto, 694-23-7.
    Leo, 694-23-9.
    Marcenia, 694-23-4.
    Margaret, 694-23-2.
    Susan, 694-23-11.
    William, 694-23-6.

L

Lambright,
    Harvey, 613.
    Hazel, 612.
Learned,
    Carl Leon, 467-16.
    Ralph Benson, 467-14.
    Thomas Alvin, 467-15.
Leiter,
    Alice V., 398.
    Charles Eugene, 400.
    Edward Thomas, 394.
    Elmer Grant, 401.
    Frances, 393.
    John William, 397.
    Lewis Henry, 396.
    Mary Jane, 395.
    Rolla Morgan, 399.

M

McBride,
    Effie, 694-22-3.
    Jason, 694-22-1.
    Maude, 694-22-4.
    Orien W., 694-22-2.
Maule,
    Ada, 508.
    Ann Elizabeth, 227.
    Charles, 513.
        " Henry, 511.
        " Lewis, 230.
        " Llewellah, 500.
    Didanna Ann, 515.
    Frank, 509.
    Jessie, 512.
    John, 510.
        " Brough, 516.
        " Ezra, 231.
    Laura Isabel, 515.
    Lillie, 506.
    Llewellah Thomas, 226.
    Lydia Margaret, 229.
    Victoria, 514.
    William Wesley, 228.
Melchoir,
    Marian Catharine, 623.
Michaels,
    Bessie, 550.
Michaels,
    Corinne, 551.
    Courtland Leroy, 546.
    John, 549.
    Margaret Eliza, 548.
    Ola Belle, 545.
    William Hallie, 547.
Miller,
    Franklin Davis, 625.
    Harry Walter, 628.
    Ida Belle, 630.
    Lillie May, 624.
    Louisa B., 694-11.
    Matthias Bartgis, 627.
    Susan Rebecca, 629.
    William Allen, 626.

N

Newcomb,
    Charlotte A., 694-22.
    Frederick, 479-20.
    Harry, 479-19.
    Hattie M., 479-23.
    Jessie M., 479-22.
    Lillie D., 479-17.
    Louis O., 479-16.
    Martha Ellen, 479-21.
    Nellie E., 479-18.
Niles,
    Rushton D., 694-24.

O

Obernderfer,
    Nellie, 666.
    William, 667.
Oram,
    Glenna, 479-37.
    Jessie, 479-36.
    Orion, 479-35.

P

Paine,
    Margaret Anne, 263.
Park,
    Anna, 522.
    Arthur Wendler, 717.
    Ezra Derr, 520.

Park,
 Harry Richmond, 716.
 Henry Rockey, 522-1.
 Hiram G., 519.
 John C., 521.
Pittman,
 Agnes Theo., 694-4.
 George Bright, 694-3.
 Martha Sophia, 694-7.
 Mary Cleone, 694-2.
 Samuel Wishard, 694-5.
 Thomas Lawrence, 694-6.
Pouder,
 David Steiner, 604.

R

Ramsburg,
 Catharine, 74.
 Clara, 200.
 Daniel Stephen, 201.
 " T., 78.
 Elias, 71.
 Elizabeth, 76.
 George Brewer, 202.
 John H., 79.
 " Thomas, 190.
 Mary, 73.
 Samuel Young, 199.
 Sophia, 75.
 Susanna, 77.
 William, 72.
 " 198.
Repp,
 Charles Wesley, 501.
 Eliza, 502.
 Jesse Cyrus, 503.
 John, 504.
 Laura Victoria, 505.
Rhodes,
 Anne Grace, 605.
 John Albert, 606.
Rice,
 Anna Othetta, 616.
 Jane Elizabeth, 618.
 Mary Louise, 617.
Rickenbaugh,
 Margaret, 722.
 Robert Berkey, 721.
Rosenberger,
 Henry Harley, 535.

Rosenberger,
 John Elmer, 536.
 Mary Alice, 534.
 William Clayton, 533.
Rowe,
 Hannah, 121.

S

Schley,
 Agnes, 381.
 Jennie, 379.
 John Reading, 642.
 Lewis Fairfax, 641.
 " Henry, 380.
 Lillian Kunkel, 640.
 Rebecca Maria, 377.
 " Steiner, 639.
 Steiner, 378.
Scholl,
 Frank, 462.
 Harry Steiner, 461.
 Lilly May, 460.
Schroeder,
 Frank J., 693.
 Harry Oscar, 692.
 Miriam, 694.
Shamberg,
 Alice Elizabeth, 727.
 David, 603.
 Henry Francis, 728.
 Mary Tacey, 729.
Shaw,
 Catharine Emily, 284.
 Charles Stoner, 281.
 Elizabeth, 287.
 George Elmer, 283.
 Henry Clay, 280.
 Howard, 286.
 Katharine Lydia, 586.
 Margaret Wolfe, 282.
 Martha, 587.
 Thomas Wilson, 285.
 Woodward Scott, 288.
Shriner,
 Edward Derr, 388.
 Shuck,
 Edgar A., 467-12.
 Kate L., 467-13.
 William C., 467-11.

INDEX.

Siebert,
    Catharine Elizabeth, 196.
    Frances, 195.
    George Todd, 197.
Snyder,
    Grace May, 706.
    Lewis W., 694-22-14.
    Mabel, 707.
    Raymond W., 694-22-13.
    Roscoe E., 694-22-11.
    Roy L., 694-22-12.
    William Raymond, 705.
Somerville,
    Alice Huldah, 571.
    Edith Lillian, 572.
Souder,
    J. Winfield, 479-3.
    John W. S., 694-8.
    Laura Belle, 479-4.
    Royal Edward, 479-5.
    William G., 479-6.
Steenberg,
    Jesse Chatfield, 479-38.
Stonebraker,
    Charles R., 193.
    Clarence Elmer, 476.
    Frances Minerva, 475.
    George William, 474.
    Horace Grant, 473.
    Minerva J., 194.
    William T., 192.
Swander,
    Clara D., 714.
    Ira A., 713.
    Nettie M., 711.
    Vernie E., 712.

T

Thompson,
    Ida Stoner, 266.
    Lucy May, 265.
Travis,
    Edie Roy, 585.
    Francis Hurlbert, 583.
    Guy Winsworth, 584.

V

Van Buskirk,
    Dorsey Rosenberger, 724.
    Helen Baker, 725.

W

Wiesenthall or Wisenall,
    Bernard Thompson, 382-1.
    Catharine, 48.
    Christian Steiner, 384.
    Daniel Church, 387.
    Elinor Jane, 386.
    Elizabeth, 47.
    Grace Bierbower, 383.
    Henry, 46.
    John, 50.
    " Bernard, 142.
    Josephine, 143.
    Maria, 49.
    Mary Catharine, 144.
    Paul, 382.
Wilcoxon,
    Clara, 438.
    Daniel C., 435.
    DeWitt Keller, 685.
    Francis M., 437.
    George, 440.
    Harry J., 439.
    Irwin Jackson, 656.
    Mary Maria, 681.
    Minette, 655.
    Myrtle, 654.
    Ruth Elizabeth, 684.
    Wilbur, 683.
    William, 436.
    " 682.
Winecaff,
    Anna, 251.
    Charles, 248.
    Emma, 250.
    William, 249.
Woodward,
    Anna, 298.
    Marcus, 299.

INDEX.

III.—Persons who have intermarried with the descendants of Jacob Steiner.

A

Allchesky, 302.
Annan, Sylvia, 396.
Ashenhurst, J. J., 185.

B

Baker, William, 97.
" Alice, 208.
Baltzell, Elizabeth, 81.
Bangheart, Henry, 694-23-1.
Bargen, Alice V., 533.
Barnhart, Sally, 65.
Barrick, Roderick A., 426.
Bartgis, Matthias E., 363.
Bartholow, Marshall, 308.
Beard, Florence, 479-10.
Bechtol, John, 164.
Bell, Catharine, 27.
Belle, Elizabeth Anne, 228.
Belle, Emma, 192.
Berkey, Julius, 240.
Best, Jane, 109.
Billy, John, 307.
Birely, Julia A., 53.
" Elizabeth, 9.
Bole, Ann, 113.
Boner, Florence, 480.
Border, D. W., 429.
Bowers, Janie, 694-23-3.
Bowlus, Ann Elizabeth, 80.
Bremer, Minnie, 479-24-4.
Brengel, Elizabeth, 7.
" Catharine, 92.
Brennan, A. F., 189-2.
Bridwell, Ann Catharine, 221.
Bright, John C., 204-1, 204-4.
Brown, Elmer, 438.
Bruchey, Sarah, 368.
" Sidney Ann, 225.
Brunner, Mary Ann, 129.

C

Campbell, Jane E., 142.
Cargill, George B., 210-10.
Carlin, Mary, 168.
Carter, John M., 195.
Clancey, Lulu A., 423.
Clemm, Enos, 126.
Clippinger, Harry, 479-18.
Clyde, W., 479-26.
Coleman, Anna A., 193.
Collins, ———, 479-36.
Colton, Ida, 344.
Conrad, W., 122.
Cover, Hannah, 205.
Craig, Narcissa, 112.
Cramer, Ethan Allen, 136.
" Rosanna, 96.
" Sophia, 731.
Crank, Thomas E., 522.
Cromwell, William, 205-1.

D

Darner, William H., 353.
Davis, Robert, 306.
Derr, John, 11.
" Thomas, 23.
Dewald, William E., 216-5.
Dick, Marion O., 89.
" Sarah, 84.
" William, 229.
Diehl, Nelson, 422.
Dilley, John, 110.
Dudrow, Mary Jane, 234.
Duffey, Loretta, 365.
Duffie, Margaret, 218.
Durbin, James, 87.

E

Eader, David, 20.
Emmert, J. A., 479-24-5.
Enos, George, 74.

F

Fackender, James M., 108.
Fallon, Margaret, 603.
Faw, Abraham, 19.
Fayman, George, 47.

INDEX.

Firestone, Oscar, 331.
Fleming, Ann V., 167.
Fogler, Mary, 37.
Fout, Isidore, 402.
" John, 85.
" Othetta Jane, 135.
Franz, Eleanor M., 519.
Frazee, John W., 210-11.
Fredericks, Henry J., 189-3.

G

Galbreath, Sadie J., 257.
Garrard, Susan E., 35.
Getzendanner, Daniel, 58.
" Jonathan, 57.
Gill, Samuel, 413.
Gittinger, Fannie Brengle, 158.
Goodrich, Eli, 694-23-4.
Graham, William, 110.
Griffith, Lida, 338.
" Maggie E., 479-24-1.
Grove, Edward Dawson, 453.
Groverman, Frances, 157.

H

Haines, Hetty A., 213.
Haller, Susan, 38.
Hamilton, David, 479-14.
Hann, A. B., 479-26-6.
Hanshew, Frederick William, 73.
Hardman, Elmer, 304.
Harnish, John E., 255.
Harrison, Agnes, 274.
Haskins, J. W., 254.
Hauser, Frederick, 28.
Hayes, T. W., 393.
Herstine, David W., 115.
Hess, Michael Edie, 107.
Hewitt, Melissa, 402.
Holbrook, Linwood Lee, 598.
Hollins, Catharine, 119.
Holmerk, Andrew, 409.
Holmes, Charles E. H., 319.
Hoover, ———, 269.
Houck, Mary, 26.
Huddleston, C., 429-26-1.
Hughes, William H., 165.

J

Johnson, ———, 444.
" J., 250.

K

Kaga, Mattie S., 237.
Keating, Cora B., 216-8.
Kegg, James M., 189-4.
Keihn, Flora, 694-22-1.
Keil, Christian, 479-26-2.
" John, 479-26-3.
Keller, Caroline M., 191.
" Carter Elizabeth, 243.
" Elizabeth C., 436.
" John William, 246.
Kelly, Eliza, 222.
Kerr, Edward F., 268.
King, Elidora May, 479-11.
" Philip, 479-25.
Kitto, John T., 67.
Klotz, Charles, 107.
Knepple, Mattie, 518.
Koogle, Harriet V., 369.
Kunkel, Lilian, 378.

L

Lambert, Lulu E., 370.
Lambright, Ann Catharine, 221.
" Samuel L., 340.
Latham, Julia, 160.
Lawrence, George R., 282.
Learned, Thomas A., 189.
Lease, Nicholas, 61.
Leighou, Sarah Catharine, 66.
Leiter, Henry, 161.
Lewis, William Henry, 217.
Link, Elizabeth, 3.
Lotta, Elizabeth, 41.
Loy, Maria Sibilla, 4.
Lugenbeel, Elizabeth, 56.

M

McBride, L. C., 479-24.
McCleery, Sadie, 290.
McNut, George, 515.
Malone, Alice G., 1891.
Manning, Elizabeth F., 412.

INDEX

Marriott, Mary E., 191.
Martin, Annie, 523.
Mast, John E., 194.
Masters, Mary, 226.
Maule, John, 95.
Melchoir, William H., 354.
Michaels, Elmira, 246.
" Leroy J., 244.
Miller, Franklin Pierce, 364.
" Julia E., 256.
" W. N., 479-9.
" William H., 379.
Morgan, Alma Jacqueline, 430.
Morrel, Martha, 479-1.
Morris, Kezia, 16.
Mull, Vienna, 516.
Mumma, Laura W., 326.
Munder, Catharine, 54.
Murray, John T., 118.
Myers, Fannie, 177.
" Jennie, 110-1.
" Sophia, 129.

N

Neal, Joseph, 67.
Needy, George, 48.
Neese, Diana, 72.
Newcomb, James, 304-7.
Nichols, Mary Jane, 230.
Niles, Charles O., 479-27-2.
Norman, Mary E., 66.

O

Oberndorfer, T. W., 414.
O'Connor, Juliet, 214.
Oram, John L., 209-1.
Orr, Florence Estelle, 351.

P

Paine, Josiah, 110.
Palmer, Aurelia Eliza, 117.
Park, C. C., 233.
Patchen, Fanny, 280.
Pettengall, Charlotte E., 162.
Pittman, Thomas, 479-2.
Plank, Elizabeth, 6.
Ponder, Charles, 322.
Pratzman, Catharine, 175.

Q

Quinn, Mary, 426.

R

Ragan, Sarah, 21.
Ramsburg, Barbara, 9.
" Belle, 425.
" Catharine Elizabeth, 2.
" Lewis, 32.
" Sebastian, 14.
" Susan, 17.
" Susannah, 12.
Rankin, Etta, 272.
" Margaret Jane, 113.
Reese, Jacob, 55.
" Irene, 339.
Repp, Adam, 227.
Rhodes, Calvin A., 325.
Rice, Thomas, 349.
Rickenbaugh, Clarence, 530.
" Frank, 531.
Riley, William, 305.
Riser, Florence, 394.
Roderick, Marietta, 208.
Rohr, Ann Elizabeth, 133.
Rosenberger, Ada, 479-36-5.
" Martha Ellen, 286.
Rowe, Thomas, 36.
Rowland, Fannie E., 276-2.
Rudy, Ellen, 30.
Russell, Sarah Ann, 109.

S

Schaeffer, Catharine E., 169.
" Jennie, 424.
Schley, Fairfax, 140.
Scholl, David M., 183.
Schroeder, Frank J., 460.
Schwab, Moses, 479-37.
Shamberg, Francis, 380.
Shaw, Thomas W., 116.
Sheffer, ———, 428.
Sherman, Mary M., 258.
Shoemaker, Sophia, 358.
Shriver, Edward, 150.
Shroyer, Minerva, 232.
Shuck, James W., 189-5.
Shukey, Francis, 276-10.

Siebert, George, 77.
Sinn, Amanda M., 181.
" Margaret, 13.
Smith, Anna Maria, 84.
" Charlotte, 89.
" Clara Virginia, 180.
Smyth, Sarah S., 139.
Snyder, John, 508.
" J. W., 479-24-7.
Somerville, Curtis, 265.
Souder, Jacob, 204-3.
" Jennie, 204-6.
Stall, Ann Broadhead, 31.
Steenberg, Eugene W., 210.
Stockman, Eva., 124.
Stonebraker, Arnold S., 75.
Swander, Edward F., 517.
Swarts, Matilda, 397.

T

Taafel, Annie E., 189-7.
Talbott, Joseph Howell, 220.
Thalheimer, Anna, 210-12.
Thomas, Anna Barbara, 4.
" Lilly. 428.
Thompson, William, 111.
Toffehmeyer, Nellie, 400.
Travis, Sylvester, 275.

V

Van Buskirk, Ralph J., 534.
Vance, Edwin, 479-17.

Vanfossen, Philip, 481.

W

Walker, E., 694-22-2.
Warner, Ann C. M., 152.
Weltzheimer, Rebecca, 42.
Wendler, Flora R., 522.
Whitney, Mary, 479-20.
Wiesenthal, Bernard, 8.
Wiest, Elizabeth, 128.
Wilcoxon, Anna Mary, 168.
" Andrew Jackson, 172.
Williams, James, 408.
Winebrenner, Margaret E., 171.
Winecaff, 104.
Wolf, Rush, 210-7.
Wolfe, Margaret, 35.
Woodward, Marcus A., 120.

Y

Yarborough, Amanda Jane, 101.
Young, May Elizabeth, 78.
" Sarah E., 174.
" Verlinda C., 169.

Z

Zimmerman, Anna May, 403.
" Catharine, 207.
Zink, Aaron, 514.
" Henry, 515.
" Lola, 710.

www.ingramcontent.com/pod-product-compliance
Lightning Source LLC
Chambersburg PA
CBHW030052170426
43197CB00010B/1495